Divine Encounters

Donna Rigney

Donna Rigney

PRESS

Dedication

*In His honor and with the help of the Holy Spirit,
I dedicate this book to Jesus, who never ceases to amaze me
with the expressions of His tender love and infinite power.*

TABLE OF CONTENTS

INTRODUCTION

Divine Encounters Begin at a Young Age

And afterward, I will pour out my Spirit on all people. Your sons and daughters will prophesy, your old men will dream dreams, your young men will see visions (Joel 2:28).

Wonder captured my eyes. Colors so bright and beautiful appeared out of nowhere. Walking towards me with arms extended was the most loving, kindest man I had ever seen. With a sparkle in His eyes and a broad smile on His lips, He invited me to come for a walk with Him. Immediately I followed, leaving those gathered around me.

Where I went I don't know; perhaps to heaven or just a place in the spirit realm. What I do know is that moment forever changed my life. I did not leave the church I was in that morning to follow my new Friend, but I did leave the natural realm, and I walked with Him into the spirit realm. For what seemed like hours but, in reality, was only a few minutes, we walked and talked together. I fell in love with this Man who knew me, cared about everything that concerned me and just wanted to spend time with me. Somehow I knew this was Jesus without Him telling me. From that moment on, all I wanted to do was see Him again, walk with Him and listen to what He wanted to tell me.

All this occurred during a typical Sunday morning church service when I was only seven years old. This experience with the Lord was so dramatic it forever shaped my life. A deep passion for His presence has never left me since that remarkable day so many years ago. After a long season of searching throughout my childhood and young adult years, the visitation I experienced with Jesus at seven resumed. With each new encounter with the Lord, instead of satisfying me, my hunger only increased for His nearness. His faithfulness to draw near to me has produced years of powerful unexpected meetings with the Lord of glory. Some of the encounters were as dramatic as visits to heaven and hell while others were prophetic in nature. These prophetic messages are for the church, the world and many concern the future.

During a period of time when the Lord guided me to simplify my life and spend most of my days with Him, His visitations and revelations increased dramatically. Daily the Holy Spirit met with me and brought me in the spirit through interactive visions and deep spiritual encounters to heaven, to hell and to the mountain of intimacy which overlooks the earth. From this spiritual mountain, He counseled me about how we could live successfully on the earth and spoke to me about future events that are coming to the world. Though I learned much from these encounters, I knew they weren't meant for me alone, but that He was giving them to me to share with others.

In the course of these sessions with the Lord, I did not physically leave the place I was in nor did I leave my body. Each and every time, the presence of the Lord came very powerfully upon me. It was not a feeling I could manufacture or duplicate. Overwhelming waves of His incredible love and a strong feeling of peace and well-being were the indicators I learned to recognize when He was present. Most of the visions I saw during these times of prayer were like watching a movie being made of Jesus and I doing something together. In these visions, I did not feel like an observer but became an active participant in all that transpired, even feeling the same emotions as one who was actually there. Throughout these encounters, Jesus always came and spoke to me by the power of the Holy Spirit and explained the meaning behind what I was seeing and experiencing.

At all times, I was completely in control of my faculties and able to end the encounter with the Lord whenever I wished, although I was never in control of what I saw or where the Lord took me. Many days I sat in prayer before Him and just enjoyed sweet fellowship with Him.

A few days before He brought me into the spirit realm on these numerous journeys, He spoke this word of direction to me: "Out of the place of communion with Me, I will birth revelation and understanding that will not only feed you. Nations will eat the bread of life that I feed you. Open yourself and share the manna I place within you. Do not be afraid of what I show you. Everything I say is necessary for the well-being of My children. Sometimes My people need good nourishing food and other times strong medicine. Trust Me, and just deliver whatever I give you through the words you will write and those you will speak. Trust Me as I reveal the depths of darkness that the enemy has awaiting My unsuspecting little ones. Believe and I will show you many more incredible things, as long as you don't doubt. Faith is the only way you can enter through the gates of divine revelation."

Through these divine encounters, I have learned that God is sovereign, and He can do whatever He wants. There is a spirit realm, just like there is a natural realm; one is not more real than the other. After Jesus died many people were allowed to see the dead raised to life.

And when Jesus had cried out again in a loud voice, he gave up his spirit. At that moment the curtain of the temple was torn in two from top to bottom. The earth shook and the rocks split. The tombs broke open and the bodies of many holy people who had died were raised to life. They came out of the tombs, and after Jesus' resurrection they went into the holy city and appeared to many people (Matthew 27: 50-53).

The people of that day saw men and women, alive and well, who had died years before and whose bodies lay deep in the ground, decayed and dismembered. These were seen with the natural eyes of those who beheld them; the spirit realm and the natural realm collided because of the resurrection power of Jesus.

Do Heaven and Hell Exist?

Many doubt the existence of an afterlife. To know of a certainty what happens when we die, we must research the Bible. This holy book speaks more distinctly and accurately on the topic of life after death than any other book. Since the Word of God was written under the inspiration of the Holy Spirit, we can be assured of its validity. No other passage in Scripture explains the truth of eternal life and the existence of heaven and hell, as well as this true story that Jesus told those sitting before Him:

> *There was a rich man who was dressed in purple and fine linen and lived in luxury every day. At his gate was laid a beggar named Lazarus, covered with sores and longing to eat what fell from the rich man's table. Even the dogs came and licked his sores.*
>
> *The time came when the beggar died and the angels carried him to Abraham's side. The rich man also died and was buried. In hell, where he was in torment, he looked up and saw Abraham far away, with Lazarus by his side. So he called to him, "Father Abraham, have pity on me and send Lazarus to dip the tip of his finger in water and cool my tongue, because I am in agony in this fire."*
>
> *But Abraham replied, "Son, remember that in your lifetime you received your good things, while Lazarus received bad things, but now he is comforted here and you are in agony. And besides all this, between us and you a great chasm has been fixed, so that those who want to go from here to you cannot, nor can anyone cross over from there to us."*
>
> *He answered, "Then I beg you, father, send Lazarus to my father's house, for I have five brothers. Let him warn them, so that they will not come to this place of torment"* *(Luke 16: 19-28).*

By means of this troubling narrative, Jesus explicitly taught that heaven and hell are real kingdoms. The Lord wants us to know the beauty and majesty of His kingdom and the horrors of Satan's.

Commissioned to Speak

Just as John the apostle did when he was exiled on the Island of Patmos, I heard the Lord tell me to write down and keep a careful record of the things He was going to reveal to me.

On the Lord's Day I was in the Spirit and I heard behind me a loud voice like a trumpet, which said: "Write on a scroll what you see and send it to the seven churches"... "Write, therefore, what you have seen, what is now and what will take place later"(Revelation 1: 10-11,19).

Unlike John, I was not exiled, nor do I claim to be writing revelations that have the validity of Scripture. But as a woman whom God has appointed to write what He often dictates to me through the inspiration of the Holy Spirit, I present these prophetic revelations to those who hunger for more.

Heaven is real and so is hell. They are as real as the earth upon which we dwell! The purpose of this book is not just to bring forth many of the inspiring revelations the Holy Spirit has given me to enrich the Body of Christ, but in addition, my desire is to instill in every reader a passion for Jesus and encourage a devotion that will make each one an ardent seeker after His glory.

For the lord your God is a consuming fire,
(Deuteronomy 4:24).

MY STORY

I have appeared to you to appoint you as a servant and as a witness of what you have seen of me and what I will show you. I am sending you to them to open their eyes and to turn them from darkness to light, and from the power of Satan to God, so that they may receive forgiveness of sins and a place among those who are sanctified by faith in me (Acts 26:16–18).

CHAPTER ONE

In Pursuit of His Glory

*I know a man in Christ who fourteen years ago was caught
up to the third heaven. Whether it was in the body or out of
the body I do not know—God knows. And I know that this
man—whether in the body or apart from the body I do not
know, but God knows—was caught up to paradise. He heard
inexpressible things, things that man is not permitted to tell
(2 Corinthian 12:2-4).*

A sudden tap on my shoulder brought me abruptly back from a
place that forever captivated my memory. For a few minutes,
I left the solemn atmosphere of the liturgical service I was attending
and had a divine encounter that dramatically changed my life.

"Hurry you will be late for Mass," my mother beckoned as
I jumped into the car with the rest of my family that memorable
Sunday morning.

Once inside the church, I left my mother's side and quietly
marched down the center aisle to the front rows where the children
sat. Feeling quite grown up at the prized age of seven years old, I slid
in the pew next to my older sister. The service was uneventful—just
like all the others I had attended with my family. We all stood when
the priest entered and prayed and sang in unison with the rest of the
congregation. Our behavior was impeccable. A kind, but very stern,
nun sat behind us making sure that we didn't disrupt the service by

talking or fooling around. When it was time to kneel, we all, like well-trained soldiers, knelt on the red cushioned kneelers.

This was when it happened. While I read my prayers in my little white missal, a beautiful man dressed in a flowing garment stood in front of me and beckoned me to come follow Him. From that moment on I was no longer in that building. I cannot tell you where I went. This wonderful man was Jesus. Together we walked through a magnificent land while He spoke tenderly to me. Whether He brought me to heaven or not, I don't know for sure, but what I found out was that He was real and that He wanted me to be His friend. He wasn't just handsome and kind; He was the most loving person I had ever met. During our brief encounter, I felt like nothing else mattered to Him but spending time with me. At seven years old I fell in love with Jesus.

Then the unthinkable happened. We had arrived at the part of the Mass where everyone had to change positions and sit down. Lost in my reverie and away in the spirit with my new Friend, I remained kneeling while all the other children sat on the bench. Leaning forward, the Sister of Mercy attending us tapped me on my shoulder and told me to sit down. Instantly I was taken out of the spirit and back into the church--and my Friend was gone. I wanted to cry and shout at being taken from Him, but I respectfully sat down and remained silent. Filled with a tremendous disappointment, I resigned myself to find Him again. From that moment on nothing else mattered to me but knowing Him.

The Quest Begins

Each and every night when I went to bed I diligently sought after Him. Kneeling beside my bed I dutifully said the prayers my mother had taught me. Then crawling between the crisp white sheets and laying my head on my pillow, I relentlessly begged Jesus to come and visit me as He had that wonderful Sunday until I grew tired and fell asleep. Hardly a night went by that I didn't ask Him to let me hear Him speak. Just hearing His gentle voice again would be enough for me. Years went by, and though I knew He was near, I didn't see Him or clearly hear His voice. I longed for His tangible presence. Knowing God and finding Him was all that mattered to me.

The years flew by and, before I knew it, I graduated junior high school and entered a Catholic high school. Every day before school I walked to the chapel in the heart of the city and went to Mass. Perhaps I would find Him there in church as I had so many years before, but it was not to happen.

Undeterred, I decided to enter the convent upon graduating from high school. I was sure that I would find my Friend there. As a Sister of Mercy every day I chanted the Office, read my Scriptures, prayed and attended Mass. All my efforts did not bring what I so longed for—His tangible presence—His glory; so after two and one half years of searching, I gave up and went home.

Though I left the convent, I didn't give up on my search. A holy determination filled my heart for a deep relationship with Jesus. Ten years later, happily married to my husband Jack, and caring for our three children, a chance encounter with a neighbor changed everything.

This congenial woman told me about a book she had read. It was the story of Pat Boone's dramatic conversion. As she explained the life changing encounter he had had with the Lord, I knew I must read this book. That night, alone with the book, my heart raced as I read Pat Boone recount a similar encounter with Jesus, one like I had when I was seven years old.

This book was all my dwindling faith needed. I knew I would find Him again. My prayer life soared. Soon after reading this book, I found a Charismatic prayer meeting held at a local church, attended it regularly, and was baptized in the Holy Spirit with the evidence of speaking in tongues. Now I was able to hear Jesus more clearly and know Him more intimately, though I still didn't see Him like I had so many years before.

Supernatural Encounters Resume

Soon after being baptized with His precious Holy Spirit, the Lord called me to pray and fast for world and church leaders. I had never fasted for an extended period of time, so I prayed about just how I was to do this. While reading the book of Daniel, I felt led to follow Daniel's example and just eat fruit and vegetables for forty days. I did this, and I have to say, it was quite easy. Even though I had to fix meals for my family daily, I was not tempted to give up the partial fast. His strength was there for me constantly during this entire time. When the forty days of prayer and fasting were up, many amazing things occurred.

Just a few days after completing the Daniel fast, two noteworthy events happened. Both Pope John Paul xxii and President Ronald Reagan were shot. Miraculously, neither was fatally wounded and both recovered completely. What a wonderful lesson I learned about the faithfulness of God. To observe firsthand how he loved these men and commissioned men and women to pray for them, deepened my devotion to Him. What a wonderful God we serve!

While thanking the Lord for sparing these wonderful leader's lives, He spoke clearly to me. During this time of prayer, He explained that, like He had done for Daniel, He was giving me the gift of interpreting dreams and visions. *And Daniel could understand visions and dreams of all kinds (Daniel 1:17).*

From that time onward, my long sought after encounters with the Lord resumed. What precious fellowship we enjoyed then and continue to enjoy to this day. He is faithful to reward those who diligently seek Him. The most precious reward He can give us is more of His presence, a deeper revelation of who He is and being submersed in His glory.

Hunger Satisfied

When I looked back upon my life, I wondered why God hid from me for such a long time. Was I not ready for more of Him? Perhaps I was not good enough? Or was there another reason that had escaped my scrutiny? Reading the account in Matthew 17:1-8 of the transfiguration of Jesus clearly revealed to me that God's ways are not our ways.

Matthew relates that Jesus led Peter, James and John up a high mountain by themselves. Once they reached the top of the mountain:

...he was transfigured before them. His face shone like the sun, and his clothes became as white as the light. Just then there appeared before them Moses and Elijah, talking with Jesus.

While he was still speaking, a bright cloud enveloped them, and a voice from the cloud said, "This is my Son, whom I love; with him I am well pleased. Listen to him!"

When the disciples heard this, they fell facedown to the ground, terrified (Matthew 17:2-6).

Wow what a tremendous divine encounter these three chosen vessels received. Why Peter, James and John? Why weren't the other nine, or even some of the faithful women, invited for this unveiling of His glory? What made these three so outstanding? Were they holier? Were they more obedient, more faithful?

Looking at what Scripture tells us about James and John, they don't appear to be any better than the rest of the disciples who followed Jesus. These were the two who asked Jesus if he wanted them to call fire down from heaven to destroy the people in the Samaritan village who did not welcome Him. At that point in their lives they were pretty volatile. Perhaps James and John were a little taken up with the power they had received from Jesus. They didn't ask Jesus to call fire down from heaven but wanted to know if they could command fire to come and destroy the village. Love—the thrust of Jesus' gospel seems to have escaped these hot-tempered brothers. (See Luke 9:51-55.)

Frequently it is reported in the Gospels that the disciples argued about who was the greatest. Pride seemed to be a strong motivating factor in their lives. James and John even went so far as to ask their mother, whom they must have thought had some influence with Jesus, to intervene for them. *She said, "Grant that one of these two sons of mine may sit at your right and the other at your left in your kingdom" (Matthew 20:21).* Peter was no better, because when he and the rest of the nine disciples heard their request, they were indignant with James and John. Jealousy, envy, pride and more than a dash of selfish-ambition were present in all of them.

So what made these three conspicuous enough for us to emulate? What quality did they possess that caught the attention of Jesus?

21

Perhaps it was their hunger for His presence. Were they not just seeking a prominent place in His kingdom for stature or did their hunger to be close to Him factor in? I believe that is the key to why they were called up the mountain to behold His glory. John was the disciple who sat right beside Jesus at the Passover dinner the night before He died. He was so close; he was able to lay his head upon Jesus' chest. (See John 13:23-25.) I wonder if James was sitting on the other side of Jesus.

Peter, too, possessed the same insatiable hunger for the tangible presence of Jesus. The story that most depicts his passion for Jesus is the one told in John 21:1-14. After Jesus' resurrection He appeared a number of times to His disciples. On one of these occasions, Peter and his friends decided to go fishing by the Sea of Tiberias. After fishing all night, they had caught nothing. In the morning Jesus appeared on the shore and told them to throw their net on the right side of the boat. Not recognizing Jesus, they followed His advice and cast their nets for one more try. Much to their amazement they caught more fish than their boat could hold, so they towed the net behind the boat toward shore.

Here's where the story reveals the heart of Peter. John, realizing that this man standing on shore was Jesus, told Peter that it was the Lord. Immediately Peter wrapped his outer garment around himself and jumped into the water. Rowing to shore was not an option. It would take too long. Peter surmised that he could reach Jesus faster if he swam. Was Pater impulsive? Yes! But that impulsive action was motivated by a deep hunger for the presence of Jesus.

I believe that it is not just the worthiness of the disciple but the depth of desire that determines the level and intensity of each divine encounter. Peter, James and John passionately loved Jesus. Their hunger grew. No matter how many times they met with Jesus, they never grew tired of His presence. Their actions proved that each encounter just wet their appetite for more of Him.

God promises to satisfy us when we hunger and thirst for righteousness. *Blessed are those who hunger and thirst for righteousness, for they will be filled (Matthew 5:6).* The deeper the desire, the greater the amount needed to fill the void. Those who just hunger a little will receive just a little, but those who's hunger and longing is enormous will receive a massive infilling.

...he rewards those who earnestly seek him (Hebrews 11:6). The Lord is good to those whose hope is in him, to the one who seeks him (Lamentations 3:25).

These are but a few of the promises in Scripture that God has given to those who seek Him. If we earnestly and wholeheartedly seek after him, He will reveal Himself to us.

...acknowledge the God of your father, and serve him with wholehearted devotion and with a willing mind, for the Lord searches every heart and understands every motive behind the thoughts. If you seek him, he will be found by you... (1 Chronicles 28:9).

Peter, James and John were God seekers. No price was too high for them to pay for His nearness: families, friends, reputations, homes, occupations. They willingly and wholeheartedly gave all in exchange for His presence, and what a tremendous encounter they experienced as they saw the glorified Jesus, Moses and Elijah and heard the voice of the Father from heaven. Because they hungered and thirsted, they were filled. What a deep hunger these three men must have had for His nearness, for God to have to lift the veil and reveal the glory of His Son to satisfy them.

I believe that one of the reasons that I had to seek after my Friend for such a long time was that He was using the years of searching to increase the hunger I had for His presence. The encounters that He had reserved for me required a deep longing for Him. The longer I searched the hungrier I got. Now I can look back at that time and thank God for it. Whatever the cost, it was worth the price. Nothing can compare to the divine encounters: not the years of searching, or the time spent in the convent, or the hours alone praying--pleading for His presence. One moment in His presence is worth a thousand elsewhere.

Who Beholds the Glory?

Is just being hungry for the divine presence all that is required to find Him in all His glory? Looking at the life of Moses, a man who experienced the presence of God like few have, we can find other attributes that are necessary. No matter how much of God he received, he was never satisfied. His hunger just grew with each encounter. That insatiable desire caused him to pursue God relentlessly. No price was too high for Moses if his portion was the glory of God.

Three months after Moses led the Israelites out of slavery in Egypt, they arrived at the Desert of Sinai. Camping there in the hot desert, Moses left the vast multitude and went up the mountain to meet with God. He entered the cloud of God's presence and stayed with God for forty days and forty nights. To the Israelites looking up where Moses disappeared into the cloud on Mt. Sinai, the glory of the Lord looked like a consuming fire.

Fear filled them, but soon they grew tired of waiting for Moses. In rebellion to exactly what God had commanded them not to do, they built a golden calf and worshiped it. As the story unfolds, God became very angry with these disobedient people that He had called His own. In frustration, God explained to Moses that He would not lead them through the desert to the Promised Land; He would send an angel to lead them the entire way.

This is where we see the heart of hunger and the persistence of Moses. Instead of thinking how cool it would be to have an angel of God leading them all the way to their Promised Land, he argued with God; an angel won't do. No, he would settle for nothing less than God's presence.

> *Then Moses said to him, "If your Presence does not go with us, do not send us up from here. How will anyone know that you are pleased with me and with your people unless you go with us?"...*
>
> *And the Lord said to Moses, "I will do the very thing you have asked, because I am pleased with you and I know you by name" (Exodus 33:15-17).*

Ordinarily this should have pleased Moses, but Moses wasn't ordinary in his pursuit of God. He apparently got what he asked God for—His presence to accompany them to the Promised Land, but Moses wasn't satisfied. He wanted more, and with great persistence he asked for it.

> *Then Moses said, "Now show me your glory."*
> *And the Lord said, "I will cause all my goodness to pass in front of you, and I will proclaim my name, the Lord in your presence. But," he said, "you cannot see my face, for no one may see me and live."*
> *Then the Lord said, "There is a place near me where you may stand on a rock. When my glory passes by, I will put you in a cleft in the rock and cover you with my hand until I have passed by. Then I will remove my hand and you will see my back; but my face must not be seen" (Exodus 33:18-23).*

Moses set a powerful example of how we can receive more of God's glory. Even after spending forty days and forty nights in God's presence, he wasn't tired of being with God. He wanted more, asked for it and received the glory.

Beholding His Face

Moses will forever be known as the man who met with God face to face. His relationship was very close with his God. We, too, can have that same relationship. Though no one can live and see the face of God with all its glory, we can, like Moses, meet with Him and behold His form with our spiritual eyes. This has often happened to me when I have been in the spirit visiting with my Lord. I have not seen His face with all its glory, but I have had glimpses of His form, seen His smile, looked into His eyes and watched Him walk ahead of me. In His mercy He has kept me from seeing Him in detail. When I have asked to see Him with greater clarity, He has explained that if I saw Him as He is I could not stand to live on the earth. The longing for Him and for heaven would be too unbearable. The visits I have experienced with our heavenly Father have had less detail than those I've experienced with Jesus, but I have seen His form, His majesty and His enormous splendor. Like Moses, the more I meet with Him, the more I desire His presence and the more I long to behold His glory.

Joshua Beheld His Glory

Moses wasn't the only one who had a deep hunger for God's presence and persistently pursued Him. When Moses left the presence of God in the tent of meeting ...*his young aide Joshua son of Nun did not leave the tent (Exodus 33:11)*. This young man loved the glory of God so much he didn't even realize that church was over. He stayed even though Moses left. How many of us stay and soak in the glorious presence of God when church is done? Even after our minister has gone home, how many stay and sit and listen for Him? Or are we like those who just stood at the entrance of their tents and watched? We can be like Joshua or we can sit looking at the clock waiting for the service to end. Our hunger will determine who we choose to be with or who we become.

Little did this young man know that as he followed the example Moses set for him and sat immersed in the glory of God, he was being prepared for a great destiny. Forty years later when Moses was getting ready for his death, Joshua was called by God to take over and lead the nation of Israel to conquer the Promised Land. Without a doubt, the courage and character necessary for this tremendous undertaking was forged in him during the years he soaked in God's glory. He absorbed the fragrance of his powerful God and with the might of the Lord led the nation. This young man became a mighty warrior and championed many victorious battles until the land was theirs as God promised.

Like Moses and Joshua, don't settle for less. Pursue! Yes, God is just waiting to see how much we want Him. He will not cast the great pearl of His glory before swine. No, He will search and find those who have a heart for Him above all else. These are the ones who will behold His glory, not just the hungry, but those who will settle for nothing less than more of Him.

Therefore, since we are receiving a kingdom that cannot be shaken, let us be thankful, and so worship God acceptably with reverence and awe, for our "God is a consuming fire" (Hebrews 12:28-29).

The Consuming Fire of His Glory

So far we have seen that we must first be hungry for God, and then second, lay aside all to pursue His presence, but is there yet another qualification that is found in those who beheld the glory of God? Isaiah prophesied about this very subject. He asked the question and gave a very specific answer so that we would have no doubt as to what God requires.

"Who of us can dwell with the consuming fire? Who of us can dwell with everlasting burning?" He who walks righteously and speaks what is right, and rejects gain from extortion and keeps his hand from accepting bribes, who stops his ears against plots of murder and shuts his eyes against contemplating evil—this is the man who will dwell on the heights, whose refuge will be the mountain fortress. His bread will be supplied and water will not fail him. Your eyes will see the king in his beauty and view a land that stretches afar (Isaiah 33:14-17).

After the requirements are listed, this wonderful promise follows: We will see the glory of God; we will see the King in all His beauty if we keep ourselves free of sin.

Therein lays the problem many of us face. Sin has a hold on our lives. If sin weren't pleasurable then it would be fairly easy to avoid, but listening to tidbits of gossip empowers our self-image and fuels our resentments. Gaining wealth through extortion or dishonesty provides material benefits without intensive labor. Illicit sexual thoughts and actions bring transitory physical pleasure. Revenge fueled by unrestrained anger satisfies our longing for retribution. Sinful pleasures are temporary but are an enticing trap nonetheless.

Sin is the bait that Satan uses in his snare to keep us from receiving the fullness of God while here on the earth and to rob us of our eternal inheritance in the afterlife. In Ephesians 6: 14 the Holy Spirit instructs us to wear the breastplate of righteousness as a shield to protect us from the devastating effects of evil. God knows if we cloak ourselves in right living, we will be protected from the devices of the evil one. Satan knows it, too! That is why he labors so diligently to draw us away from God and into his trap of sin.

We must be alert and watch out for the bait that he presents to us daily: bitter resentful thoughts, sexual fantasies, lies to escape the price of truth, rebellion against those who are over us, laziness and slothfulness instead of diligence in executing our responsibilities. These are but a few of the devices he uses to draw us into sin, and he knows which bait to use to set an effective trap for each one of us. Those who are hard workers won't grab the bait of laziness but perhaps sexual fantasies or a gossip session with a friend will.

God's Word warns us not to give the devil any place in our lives, not even a foothold:

> *Therefore each of you must put off falsehood and speak truthfully to his neighbor, for we are all members of one body. "In your anger do not sin": Do not let the sun go down while you are still angry, and do not give the devil a foothold. He who has been stealing must steal no longer, but must work, doing something useful with his own hands, that he may have something to share with those in need (Ephesians 4:25-28).*

If righteousness is a shield that protects and a prerequisite to receive God's glory, then be assured, Satan will try to remove it from us. He will dangle bait in front of us that will attract us. If we grab the bait and sin and loose our impenetrable shield of righteousness, then we give Satan or his demons the legal right to come into our lives to steal, kill and destroy.

Thank God that Jesus provided a way of escape and a way to be set free from those sins that so easily beset us—the precious blood of the Lamb.

His Glory Will Change the World

While I was contemplating the damage sin does to our lives and the barrier it erects between us and God, the Lord visited me with an interactive vision: I saw the Lord sitting on an elaborately embossed throne. Cobwebs of time hung around it. The Lord had been waiting quite a while for me to enter the deep place within where He abides. Enthusiastically He jumped to His feet and stepped off His throne and then beckoned me to follow Him.

He declared, "You have been observing the soot and dirt that sin produces. Now come! I want to show you the benefits that come to those who leave their sin and follow Me." I saw shimmering gems, diamonds and glistening gold. All were displayed in an atmosphere void of dust and dirt and replete with joy. Music—a festive, glorious melody filled the expanse we visited.

"Few find these places, for many are not willing to pay the price to enter the expanse of blessings," my Friend explained. "Holiness, right living, hatred and rejection of all that is evil: that is the way to enter this place of divine encounters. No other attitude will allow entrance."

He continued: "It is My presence that changes your world. I am the God who walked in the fiery furnace and changed a fiery tomb into a platform for proclaiming the truth and bringing forth a grand, glorious promotion. It is My presence that shuts the mouth of the lion. Instead of being a meal for hungry lions, Daniel served a meal of My greatness to an entire nation. Death and destruction disappeared in My presence and was changed into revival and promotion.

"My presence changed Elijah's life as well. Evil prophets were destroyed and a great revival ensued, for My presence brings change. It is My presence that must be sought if any change is to come into your lives and your nation. Seek Me daily until you find Me.

"You cannot be a friend of the world and a friend of God. There must be a separation in order for there to be a connection. Either you will be separated from your God and connected to the world, or you will be separated from the world and connected to your God. You cannot have it both ways. Be in the world but not of the world.

Hate what the world loves: immorality, greed, theft, manipulation, selfish ambition...

"Love Me and love My ways, and My presence will change your life. That is how you will experience My power. Alone, separated from the world and gathered together in worship and prayer: that is where My Spirit fell at Pentecost. Be ye separate like Daniel: not eating the world's manna (teachings); not worshiping the gods of this world expecting them to help you; not falling down and worshiping your leaders; not bowing before the idol of religious activity but bowing in humility in intimate communion toward your God. My presence brings revival."

The Lord will be found by all who seek hard after Him. Obedience brings the greatest reward! As He woes, as He beckons and we respond in obedience, our reward will be great. Moses, Daniel, the three Hebrew men, Elijah, Peter, James and John all pursued God and He allowed them to catch Him; how great was their reward! They beheld the glory. They paid the price: hunger for God, pursuing God in obedience and living a righteous life.

He concluded our meeting by emphasizing the importance of this truth: "An encounter with Me is what the world needs. An encounter with Me is what the lost need. An encounter with Me is what your children and loved ones need. Cry out to Me on their behalf, and I will answer with My presence."

CHAPTER TWO

The Seer Anointing Explained

And afterward, I will pour out my Spirit on all people. Your sons and daughter will prophesy, your old men will dream dreams, and your young men will see visions (Joel 2:28).

On September 24, 1992, three prophets assembled at the non-denominational church I was attending to prophesy the Word of the Lord over some members of the congregation who had been previously selected for this honor. To my great excitement, I was included in this fortunate group. One of the prophets began speaking over my life and prophesied that God would be using me as a seer in the years to come. This information should have delighted me, but it just caused me to wonder. At this time I had never heard of a seer and did not understand what God was calling me to do.

Since then I have learned that a seer is someone who has the gift of prophecy. What makes them different than other prophets is that their gifts flow more in the realm of the visual. Rather than just hearing words spoken to them, a seer sees visions or has dreams which the Holy Spirit then interprets. These messages are usually given to exhort, to encourage, to instruct or to warn those to whom the seer is led.

There are many examples in Scripture that verify the validity of the seer anointing. The book of Daniel is filled with references of the interpretation of dreams and visions. This is one of the gifts that Daniel operated in to a truly miraculous degree. *And Daniel could understand visions and dreams of all kinds (Daniel 1:17).* King Nebuchadnezzar threatened to have all the wise men in Babylon killed if they could not give him the meaning of a dream he had dreamt. Not only did he want the interpretation, but he also wanted them to relate exactly what the dream was because he wanted to be sure he was getting the proper interpretation.

Daniel went in to see the king and asked for more time so that he might reveal and interpret the dream. During the night, Daniel received a vision from the Lord explaining the mysterious dream. The next day, giving all the glory to God, he explained to the king, first the dream in detail, then the interpretation, after which, all the lives of the wise men in Babylon were spared. The King declared that Daniel's God is the God of gods, and he appointed Daniel as one of the rulers over the entire province of Babylon. What wonderful miracles God preformed through the seer anointing on Daniel. (The full story is found in Daniel 2.)

The dreams and visions and the interpretations all come from God, and only He can reveal the mysteries hidden in them. Truthfully Daniel told King Nebuchadnezzar, *"No wise man, enchanter, magician or diviner can explain to the king the mystery he has asked about, but there is a God in heaven who reveals mysteries" (Daniel 2:27-28).*

Like Daniel, I have learned not to try to figure out the dreams or visions I receive but to bring them before the Holy Spirit. He is always faithful to bring me the understanding I need, because He is the revealer of all mysteries.

Another person truly gifted as a seer was Joseph. As a boy he received two dreams. (See Genesis 37:5-11). Because of his zeal and immaturity, he told his jealous brothers these dreams which depicted him ruling over them someday. The premature unveiling of these dreams to the wrong people caused Joseph many problems. Joseph's brothers sold him into slavery. Brought to Egypt, he eventually ended up in prison there for many years.

A premature delivery of a dream got Joseph enslaved and imprisoned, but a divinely inspired interpretation of a dream was the key God used to get him released. The Pharaoh ruling Egypt had a very disturbing dream. When he found out that Joseph could interpret dreams, he sent for him to be released from prison and brought before him. Just like Daniel, Joseph humbly told the Pharaoh when he asked him to interpret the dream: *"I cannot do it...but God will give Pharaoh the answer he desires" (Genesis 41:16).*

After the Holy Spirit had given the interpretation of the dream through Joseph to Pharaoh, the man who was held as a prisoner in a dungeon was released and promoted. Realizing that God was with Joseph Pharaoh exclaimed, *"Since God has made all this known to you, there is no one so discerning and wise a you" (Genesis 41:39).* Then he placed Joseph in charge of the whole land of Egypt. The King alone ruled over Joseph.

Knowing and obeying God, spending time in His presence, receiving revelation and understanding from Him brought Daniel and Joseph from a place of captivity to a place of leadership. I have always loved their stories and wanted to know God like they did. It is wonderful to see visions, dream dreams and receive the interpretations of them, but it is a far greater thing to know the God who speaks through these dreams and visions.

Isaiah was such a man. At the onset of his ministry as a prophet, Isaiah saw an incredible vision. He saw, *The Lord seated on a throne, high and exalted, and the train of his robe filled the temple (Isaiah 6:1).* Oh, what a blessed man he was! The heavens were opened before him, and he saw the Lord in all His glory because he was one who sought after God.

The character of Isaiah is revealed when we see his response to this heavenly vision: *"Woe to me!"..."I am ruined! For I am a man of unclean lips..." (Isaiah 6:5).* Instead of thinking how great he must be because he was chosen to see God, his immediate reaction was one of humility. Yes, he sought after God, but he knew he was a man who had sinned. He realized that he did not deserve to see this vision of the Lord.

Isaiah was a man deeply in love with God and willing to lay aside everything to serve Him. He was not a distant God to Isaiah but a friend and companion whom he revered and trusted. When the Lord spoke to him and asked, *"Whom shall I send? And who will go for us?" (Isaiah 6:8).* Immediately, with no thought of the sacrifice or the persecution that serving God would bring to him,

Isaiah responded, *"Here am I. Send me!"(Isaiah 6:8)*. Here was a man set apart for God, chosen by Him to be a prophet and seer. All he wanted was to speak for his God, because he loved Him more than his own life.

Isaiah's life and enormous devotion to the Lord has inspired many to know God and speak His messages, whether they come as dreams, visions or prophetic words. These are days not much different from those that Isaiah lived in, and God desires to speak to His people. He still chooses some to be His spokesmen. Let it be our deepest desire to be selfless and courageous like Isaiah and to never withhold His word for fear of reprisals, but to speak simply because we love Him and He's our friend.

When I think of friends of God, I think of Jeremiah who lived around 600 BC. He was called by God as a young man: *"Before I formed you in the womb I knew you, before you were born I set you apart; I appointed you as a prophet to the nations" (Jeremiah 1:3)*.

Even though Jeremiah responded, *"Ah Sovereign Lord, I do not know how to speak; I am only a child" (Jeremiah 1:6)*, the Lord convinced him to accept the call. Like a devoted father, God told Jeremiah that He would rescue him and put His words in his mouth.

After his commissioning, Jeremiah saw two visions which the Lord interpreted for him. Jeremiah needed to know what the branch of an almond tree and the boiling pot tilting away from the north represented. He did not have to strive for an understanding of what he saw but was given the meaning of both visions without even asking. The Lord wonderfully equips His prophets with all they need to fulfill His will. It truly is an awesome thing to serve the God of all the nations.

Ezekiel, too, had the great honor of being called by God to speak on His behalf. He, like Isaiah and Jeremiah, saw visions of God. (See Ezekiel 1:1.) The visions he saw were magnificent and recorded in detail throughout the book of Ezekiel.

Suffering and depravation marked Ezekiel's life, but his devotion to God was unwavering. The dreams, visions and words he received did not sustain him during the multitude of trials he endured, but his loving relationship with his God did. He never took his eyes off the Almighty God he served. His focus was not on the people about him, his exile to Babylon and captivity there, nor his gifts and calling; his gaze stayed fixed on his God alone.

Over and over again the Lord spoke His message to His friends using dreams and visions. Daniel, Joseph, Isaiah, Jeremiah and Ezekiel are but a few men found in the pages of the Old Testament whose eyes were opened to see things as He sees them.

Dreams and Visions in the New Testament

The New Testament is also filled with examples of men and women who had dreams, saw visions, and heard messages from the Lord. Many of them were clearly led out of dangerous situations. Some were given specific instructions through these encounters. Others received teaching and revelations for the church, as well as for themselves, from these dreams and visions. The seer anointing continued to flow before Jesus' birth, throughout His life and after His resurrection and ascension.

Joseph, the devoted husband of Mary and foster father of Jesus, had three such dreams. In the first dream an angel appeared to him and told him it was alright to marry Mary. He was considering putting her away quietly, because she was pregnant prior to their union. The angel also told him that the child, who was to be named Jesus, was conceived by the Holy Spirit. Joseph took Mary to Bethlehem where she gave birth to Jesus.

While he and his family were in Bethlehem, an angel appeared to him in a second dream. This angel warned Joseph to take Jesus and Mary to Egypt, because Herod wanted to kill the child. Immediately Joseph obeyed the message that came to him through the angel as he slept. He went to Egypt and waited there, because the angel promised he would tell him when Herod was dead.

After Herod died, as was promised, the angel again came to Joseph and told him to return to Israel. Step by step Joseph was led by God through dreams to his destiny, out of harm's way and back to his homeland.

After Jesus' ascension back to heaven, one of his disciples, while being persecuted for his faith in the Lord saw an open vision...

Stephen, full of the Holy Spirit, looked up to heaven and saw the Glory of God and Jesus standing at the right hand of God. "Look" he said, "I see heaven open and the Son of Man standing at the right hand of God" (Acts 7:55-56).

His eyes were opened. He saw where he was going, for in just a few minutes, he was stoned to death. This vision gave him the faith to persevere through the painful death he endured. Stephen embraced the reality of this open vision, and with it, the promise of the glory he would share with Jesus.

Many times God will give His children a dream, vision or word to encourage us and to let us know that there is a light at the end of the tunnel. I've learned that what He shows us is the truth. Yes, we might be suffering for a season, but the reality is whatever He reveals to us. He didn't show Steven a vision of him pummeled with rocks; He showed him heaven, his home coming, his eternal reward.

Saul, a murderous enemy of the Lord's, saw a vision and heard from Jesus so powerfully that he was transformed into one of God's greatest apostles. While on the road to Damascus, he saw a light from heaven flash around him. He fell to the ground, heard Jesus speak to him and from that moment was never again the same man. Ananias, a man sent by God through a vision, went to Saul. Also in a vision, Saul was told that a man named Ananias would come to him, pray for him, and he would receive his sight back. Ananias obeyed and the words spoken through the vision were fulfilled. Saul saw again, but this time when his eyes were opened, he saw the world as God sees it. Saul, also known as Paul, became an apostle, a gifted teacher, prophet and seer. (See Acts 9:1-19.)

Paul wasn't the only apostle who saw visions. Peter was given a vision that taught him that God accepts everyone no matter what nation they come from, as long as they fear and obey Him. Before that visual revelation, Peter was bound by the Jewish laws and customs. After that teaching encounter, he was free to extend God's liberty and grace to all. (See Acts 10; 9-48.)

Philip, too, was greatly used by the Lord with miraculous signs. (See Acts 8; 4-8.) In a vision, he was directed by an angel to travel down a certain road. Obeying the angel, he ministered the gospel to the Queen of Ethiopia's high official on the road to Gaza. After baptizing the man, Philip was suddenly taken away and appeared at another town, Azotus.

John saw visions like Paul and Ezekiel. The Book of Revelation, which he wrote under the inspiration of the Holy Spirit, is filled with mystical visions and divine encounters. He, like Paul and many others, visited the third heaven.

God has much to say and abundantly more to do through His people. His work is not complete; He is using people today who will let Him use their lives just as He did years ago.

How to Interpret Dreams and Visions

Early one morning the Lord spoke to me and showed me how great His desire is to lead His children using dreams and visions:

"My child, when I speak to you through a dream, I am giving you a picture of how I see things. Remember whatever I say is truth. I do not lie or exaggerate. Believe what I show you and others in dreams. You are going to hear more reports of people having vivid dreams. Believe what I say through these dreams. This is the day the prophet Joel spoke about when he said I would be pouring My Spirit out on all people, that old men will dream dreams (see Joel 2:28). Yes, all people! Many will hear the word of the Lord through dreams and visions. The prophets will prophesy. Listen, heed the words I speak, and obey whatever I tell you. Dreams are not figments of your imagination but are avenues through which I teach My children the truth."

Before I begin sharing some of the mysteries the Lord directed me to reveal, I would like to briefly explain a few things I have learned about interpreting dreams and visions. Those of you that are reading this book might have had similar experiences and have not fully understood them. Also I would like to take some of the mystery out of the subject of dreams, visions and hearing from God.

I believe one of the reasons that the Lord uses pictures to reveal His thoughts are because one picture can speak a thousand words. The simplest vision can speak volumes to us. The colors, the people, every detail means something and reveals God's heart to us.

Because the Lord knows us perfectly, He sometimes speaks through dreams and visions so we won't forget what He wants to show us. Pictures are easier for some of us to remember. It has often happened that after hearing a word from the Lord, I find that I inadvertently forget it in a few days or weeks. When He speaks to me in dreams or visions, I remember them for years. These vivid messages, once interpreted, have had a long lasting impact on my life.

Frequently the Lord cannot get our full attention during the day because we are 'busy about many things,' so while we are asleep, and He has our undivided attention, He uses dreams to speak to us.

I know that not all dreams are God inspired. Some come from our sub-conscious or are influenced by what we've eaten before going to sleep, but I do believe that many dreams do come from the Lord. More than we are aware of,

> *For God does speak-now one way, now another-though man may not perceive it. In a dream, in a vision of the night, when deep sleep falls on men as they slumber in their beds, He may speak in their ears and terrify them with warnings, to turn man from wrongdoing and keep him from pride, to preserve his soul from the pit... (Job 33:14-18).*

In order to determine if a dream I had is from the Lord, I ask Him to help me remember it clearly. Usually if it is 'just me' the dream fades from my thoughts. Once I have determined that the dream is from the Lord, I write it down in detail. I also write how I felt, my emotional state during the dream. Generally the dreams are for the person dreaming. I take note of what is going on in my life and see how the dream applies to it. Then I pray and ask the Lord for the interpretation. Sometimes I am led to look up some of the objects that are in the dream in the book, *Understanding the Dreams You Dream* by Ira Milligan. This book is wonderful and has greatly enhanced my understanding of what some of the things, places, and people symbolize in the dreams I receive.

After I have researched the symbols, if I feel led to, I then begin the most important step. I sit with the Holy Spirit, pen and journal in hand, and write what He shows me the dream meant. Remember

He gives the dreams, and He alone knows what He is saying through them.

Some dreams are purely symbolic. This is easy to tell because nothing is factual, or like reality in the dream. There are times when the dream is literal, or exact, and needs no interpretation. For example, one night I dreamt that one of my children, while on the way to work, got in a head-on collision with an oil truck on a road she traveled to and from work. Immediately upon waking, I began praying for her and against the accident. After praying for a while, I felt a peace about it and went back to sleep. That morning my daughter called me and told me of "a really weird thing that happened" to her on her way to work. You guessed it! An oil truck almost hit her head-on, as she was going around a dangerous curve! She could not explain how the truck missed her. That is an example of a dream that is just taken as it is, a factual dream that was a warning and a call to pray.

A common mistake to avoid in interpreting dreams is to take as factual part of a symbolic dream. For example, if the dream is about your husband and nothing in the dream is truly as it is, then you have to find out who your husband represents in that specific dream. The Holy Spirit might be showing you the relationship Jesus, the husband of the Church, wants with you. Other people and places in your dream need to be brought before the Holy Spirit to find out who or what they really represent.

When I wake up remembering a dream, I feel a great responsibility to find out what the Lord is telling me. He loves us dearly, and just like any loving father would, He is faithful to instruct, warn, correct and encourage us. My prayer is that your ears will be ever open to hear the loving words of your Dad and that the eyes of your understanding will be open to His truth.

Commissioned to Write

These are the words that the Lord spoke to me when He directed me to reveal our encounters: "Will you share My love faithfully even when other things absorb your thoughts? Will you remember these encounters and the rich deposit of My great love that I have freely given you? Will you faithfully speak words that will turn the hearts of men to Me? Will you speak the truth even when skeptics look upon you with unbelief? Will you write the words and explain the visions knowing they will bring you persecution? Will you do it for love of Me? Will you believe steadfastly that I have spoken to you and opened your eyes to see what few have been allowed to see?"

Very seriously He continued: "If you can say yes to these requests, then follow Me to your full inheritance; walk hand in hand with Me to fulfill the call on your life. No man has chosen you nor appointed you to this work. My hand has picked you and set you apart to walk this path of revelation. Receive revelation and reveal the truth, and your joy will be complete!"

Write down the revelation and make it plain on tablets so that a herald may run with it (Habakkuk 2:2).

Now in obedience to His call on my life, I present the remaining chapters of *Divine Encounters* which are filled with the written testimony of our divine encounters. My prayer is that they will inspire all who read them to get apart with Him so that each one will see, hear and know Him as He is. Remember though the Lord calls us to be holy or set apart for Him, it is not just a matter of worthiness, but the depth of desire and of faith that determines the level and intensity of each divine encounter.

Then I heard the voice of the Lord saying, "Whom shall I send? And who will go for us?" And I said, "Here am I. Send me!" He said, "Go and tell this people" (Isaiah 6:8-9).

DESCENDING INTO HELL

Then I saw a great white throne and him who was seated on it. Earth and sky fled from his presence, and there was no place for them. And I saw the dead, great and small, standing before the throne, and books were opened. Another book was opened, which is the book of life. The dead were judged according to what they had done as recorded in the books. The sea gave up the dead that were in it, and death and Hades gave up the dead that were in them, and each person was judged according to what he had done. Then death and Hades were thrown into the lake of fire. The lake of fire is the second death. If anyone's name was not found written in the book of life, he was thrown into the lake of fire (Revelation 20:11-15).

CHAPTER THREE

My Descent into the World of Darkness

*The hand of the Lord was upon me, and he brought me out
by the Spirit of the Lord and set me in the middle of a valley;
it was full of bones. He led me back and forth among them,
and I saw a great many bones on the floor of the valley
(Ezekiel 37: 1-2).*

Sitting quietly while meditating on His Word, the Lord's presence
came mightily upon me. Though I was accustomed to His sweet
presence, this particular morning His love felt more tangible and left
me breathless. Little did I know what He had in store for me that day,
or in the days ahead, or how tremendously it would affect my life?

My Introduction to Hell

During this dramatic encounter with Jesus, the Lord took me by
the hand and led me to a very high place in the spirit realm overlooking a steep cliff. As I advanced towards the cliff, I watched in
horror while many people fell off the ominous cliff into a deep, vast
darkness below. A number of them hung onto the sides at the edge of
the precipice. Jesus urged me to run over and lift those clinging on
for dear life back onto the side of the mountain and keep them from
falling to the sure place of death beneath them.

Jesus spoke clearly as I pulled many to a place of safety: "I know that you do not want to believe in the reality of hell. To pretend it is not there, or that it is just a place that very evil people go to when they die is not the truth. My child, many do not find the path to life and others do not stay upon it once they find it. There are only two roads in life: one leads to heaven and eternal life, the other leads to hell and eternal death. Many, I say again, many are thrown into the pit of eternal suffering and pain daily. They are in need of a rescuer that will leave everything behind and run to their rescue. For this reason I have called you and set you apart: to save the lost by My power and in My strength. Keep your eyes on Me; listen as I lead you, and many souls will be saved. You have been called for such a time as this."

Many months passed before my Friend took me back to the entrance into hell. Even though I hadn't revisited this dark place, the memory of people falling into the land of torment and despair lingered. Because of this brief encounter at the precipice of hell, a stark change gripped my life. A sincere passion to reach the lost was birthed in me. My prayer life took on a new focus; now I prayed diligently for all mankind to meet their Savior. Not only was my prayer life impacted, but my actions reflected this change as well. Frequently and without difficulty, I was able to speak to those I encountered about Jesus. Many repented for their sins and accepted His gift of eternal life. Hell had become very real to me, and I did my best to rescue as many as possible from going there.

The Cobblestones of Hell

Months after this life changing revelation of people being dragged into hell, my Lord visited me. Our encounter was not any different than those I had grown accustomed to. My Friend appeared and a shower of His love instantly saturated my being. Looking into my eyes, He took my hand in His and became very serious. I recalled the last time He had such a somber tone in His voice: It was the day He brought me to the entrance to hell.

In the past twenty-five years, I had grown accustomed to my visits with Jesus. Frequently He brought me on wonderful spiritual journeys. He always used these encounters to teach me a truth or to bring a deeper revelation to me of who He is, but this day was different.

With deep affection and overflowing compassion, the Lord continued to prepare me for what I was about to see on this spiritual excursion. Gently He explained that it was imperative for me to go where He was about to take me. He wanted me to fully understand why this revelation I was about to encounter was so important to Him. My Lord wanted it to be just as important to me as it was to Him; it was to become my quest in life. Filled with wonder at His words, I went off on my spiritual passage with Jesus.

As in many other visions in the past, I saw an enormous eagle come and beckon me to climb on his back. *...but those who hope in the Lord will renew their strength. They will soar on wings like eagles (Isaiah 40:31)*. Together the friendly eagle and I flew to what appeared to be a high mountain. After landing on the mountain, I climbed down and went and sat alone upon a small patch of green grass. Curiosity welled within me and prompted me to walk over to the edge of what I thought was a cliff to see what I hoped and imagined would be a beautiful sight. To my complete amazement, I saw a very enormous place of great darkness. Huge, ugly, black birds, unlike anything found on the earth, were flying out of this dark, ominous place. Instinctively I realized that I was back at the entrance to hell.

To my great relief, the Lord appeared beside me and with His arm around my shoulder; He explained why He brought me back to the entrance of hell. Fear and revulsion overcame me while I listened to Him tell me that He was taking me down to see the place of torment the enemy has prepared for so many. This spiritual journey into Satan's domain was crucial so that I would have a greater desire, a passion within me to keep His children out of here. Feeling upset, but at the same time understanding why it was so important for my Friend to show me this terrible place, I sat on the edge of the cliff and began my descent into hell.

While climbing down the steep, black embankment, I reached for something to hold onto. Instantly I felt metal rungs for my hands and feet to use as I climbed slowly down into the darkness. While descending on this strange stairway, I reached out and felt the wall the metal rungs were fastened to. The wall was cold, wet and oddly shaped. I asked the Lord what I was feeling; He explained that the enemy loved to counterfeit the works of God. Satan had the walls of hell built with the body parts of the people he dragged there. ...*you also, like living stones, are being built into a spiritual house to be a holy priesthood (1Peter2:5).* He took the Lord's blueprint for His Kingdom and tried to duplicate it in his. What a horrible distortion of the Word of God I felt beneath my hand.

As I carefully descended, suddenly out of nowhere, I saw bodies falling or being thrown into this deep pit. In the distance, I heard piercing screams and loud moans. This place was like nothing I had ever seen on my previous encounters with Jesus. After reaching the bottom of this wall I had climbed down, I stood still, terrified at what I saw and heard. Shocked at the size of this place that I thought was a hole or a deep pit, I entered into a vast land. My fear reached such a height that I became paralyzed by it. I told the Lord I could not go on. He took me in His arms and said He would carry me, but I must see what He had to show me.

As I stood resting in His arms He said, "My presence makes all this bearable. No matter what you face that frightens you, instead of running away, run to Me and My presence will sustain you."

Then standing bravely beside Him, with my hand in His, we walked together into the darkness of hell. There was no green grass here, no beautiful flowers or butterflies. I noticed a complete absence of all things good and beautiful. As I walked forward, I knew that I walked upon multitudes who were used as the cobblestones of hell's floor ...*those who descend to the stones of the pit. Like a corpse trampled underfoot... (Isaiah 14:19).*

"Oh Lord, this place is so horrible. I can't stand to walk on these people," I cried out to my Friend. As I complained, we began climbing up grey cobblestone steps that led to a large amphitheater like arena.

Enter through the narrow gate. For wide is the gate and broad is the road that leads to destruction, and many enter through it. But small is the gate and narrow the road that leads to life, and only a few find it.

Not everyone who says to me, "Lord, Lord," will enter the kingdom of heaven, but only he who does the will of my Father who is in heaven (Matthew 7:13-14, 21).

Satan's Arena of Horror

...your breath is a fire that consumes you. The people will be burned as if to lime; like cut thorn bushes they will be set ablaze (Isaiah 33:11-12).

Shockingly the new area we entered resembled the stadiums of ancient Rome where the Christians were killed by lions. The thing that made this arena so terrible was that the area inside, around which the seats encircled, was a fiery pit. I saw demons screaming and cheering as souls were being thrown by other humans into the fire. Amazed at what I saw, I asked Jesus what was happening. He told me that many of the demons who ruled over the souls here were very lazy. Because of their slothfulness, they made the souls in hell torture each other. In disbelief I watched people drag other tortured souls by chains, all the while being screamed at by the demons controlling them. Whether they wanted to or not, they were made to abuse their fellow prisoners.

The Lord explained that this was where Satan prepared his lively building stones for the structures he and his demons created in hell. The bodies were being stripped of all impurities in this fire. Hair, eyeballs, flesh and organs were being burned away in this fire. Demons poked at the bodies and stirred them with long, metal, fork-like objects from the observation area of the stadium. All the time they laughed and howled hideously. The more the people in the pit of fire screamed in pain, the louder the demons laughed. New bodies were continuously being thrown into this pit by those humans who had been set aside for this 'privilege' by Satan himself.

Taking on the Characteristics of Evil

The more they threw people into the pit, the more these souls began to resemble the demons that controlled them. Similarly the hatred of the demons for these lost souls became contagious, and the demon's assistants became increasingly filled with the same hatred. Once their hatred reached a realm that satisfied the demons, they were replaced by other assistants. Immediately they were then cast into the same pit where they had previously so eagerly thrown their comrades. The smell of burning flesh filled the air and sickened me. As I looked around the arena, I saw great hordes of demons laughing and screaming. They were thoroughly enjoying the amusement that Satan had provided for them. Horrified in unbelief, I asked the Lord if what I was observing was really true.

Gently He responded: "Yes, My daughter, sadly to say this is very true. This is why I am so desperate for you to bring My message to My people. I cannot bear that any would come to this place of horror. It must become real to you so that nothing will stop you from warning My children. Daughter, I need you to hear, see and know the truth, not just of My kingdom but also of the kingdom of Satan. You must know the whole truth, the entire gospel, if you are to preach it effectively. Continue to walk with Me, My child."

I remembered the words Jesus spoke in Scripture:

> *If your hand causes you to sin, cut it off. It is better for you to enter life maimed than with two hands to go into hell, where the fire never goes out (Mark 9:43-44).*

Today, in the spirit, I saw that never-ending fire.

I felt nauseous and faint from what I had encountered here so far, but I knew if I left the spirit realm I would have to return at another time to see what My Lord wanted to show me. It was better to get it over with, so I continued with my hand in Jesus'. As we left the arena, I dreaded what I would see next.

The Garden of Darkness

> *Anyone who claims to be in the light but hates his brother is still in the darkness. Whoever loves his brother lives in the light, and there is nothing in him to make him stumble. But whoever hates his brother is in the darkness and walks*

*around in the darkness; he does not know where he is going,
because the darkness has blinded him (1 John 2:9-11).*

Walking timidly through the oppressive darkness, my Friend gently led me into an outer area that looked like a garden, only there was nothing alive in it. I saw bodies strewn all over the ground, lying in piles, moaning and screaming in pain. Black demon-vultures flew down and tore flesh off the bodies that were struggling to get away from these vicious birds. In utter dismay I realized that none of the victims of this torture got up and attempted to run away.

Suddenly a loud voice cried out in the darkness, "They are chained here by their brothers!" An evil laugh followed. As I observed this fearful scene, I knew that Satan was mocking Jesus by duplicating the Garden of Gethsemane. Looking up at Jesus, seeing the pain in His expression, instantly His sorrow became mine. I felt the deep pain that He endured in this place of horror.

My heart broke as the Lord revealed the depths of His sorrow: "My heart grieves for each one lying here being tortured by these vultures. I don't see the sins that brought them here, but I see what they were meant to become in My Father's kingdom. I died so that they would not. I suffered in the Garden of Gethsemane, so they would not have to come to the garden of Satan himself.

"Everyone," He continued, "everything that comes into Satan's kingdom is used by him for evil purposes. There is no good found in him."

My Lord cautioned: "Tell My children to stay away from him and his evil devices. He is a master of trickery and deception. Look how he is deceiving the ones he chooses to help him in his torture chamber. As they become more and more like him, they are deceived into thinking they will escape the fire they have thrown others into. Little do they know they are part of the sport he uses to entertain his demons? Their hatred for their fellowman delights the demons until they grow tired of them and then they become the next victims. His devices are many. Warn My children, My daughter."

The Victimizer Becomes the Victim

Painfully He explained: "The tactics you have seen Satan use in his kingdom are the same that he uses on the earth. He makes brother turn against brother. The very hatred he fosters in the hearts of My children for one another is the weapon he uses to destroy them. Cancers break out in those whose hearts are filled with hatred. Mental illness and addictions torment those whose lives have been taken over by jealousy and contempt. The victimizer eventually becomes the victim. Hatred, anger, jealousy, bitterness and fear are some of his favorite weapons of destruction."

As I stood beside Jesus and surveyed Satan's garden, I realized this was a place of perpetual darkness. There was no light shining here, but a dark mist covered this garden. Despair hung like a blanket over everyone and everything. The only sounds I heard were the cries of anguish from the people being devoured by the demon-vultures. Many tried to escape from the talons and mouths of these beasts by hiding under the bodies of those chained beside them, but not one offered themselves as a covering for another. I could hear them say, "If I have to suffer, why shouldn't you?"

Each one suffered alone with no support from anyone near them. This intensified the suffering of everyone lying on the black dirt of this evil garden. Large maggots that came up from the ground tore at the flesh the vultures couldn't reach, magnifying the pain of each poor suffering soul.

And if your eye causes you to sin, pluck it out. It is better for you to enter the kingdom of God with one eye than to have two eyes and be thrown into hell, where "their worm does not die, and the fire is not quenched" (Mark 9:47-48).

As I watched in stark horror, I saw a continuous stream of people being dragged into the garden and chained to the ground in whatever position they landed, as their captors emotionlessly served the demons directing them. Despair was everywhere. There was no hope of escape for anyone.

Looking closer at these demon vultures, I saw large, sharp fangs dripping with the blood of their chained victims. The more they ingested the blood of these people the larger, stronger, and more vicious they became. It seemed like these demons had a personnel contest going on amongst them. Whoever destroyed the most bodies would win the honor of being the chief among the demons in this section of hell. They often fought with each other over the new bodies that the human helpers dragged in.

I noticed that a few of the demon-vultures became aware of Jesus' presence. When they saw Him they hid their faces under their wings. They could not look upon Him.

Placing His arm around my shoulder, with loving approval in His eyes, He beckoned me; "It's time to go, My friend. I have more to show you. Don't be afraid. The demons you see can't touch you. They know you are Mine. Observe what I show you, so that many will know the truth and escape these horrors."

Walking hand in hand as we left Satan's garden, or rather, torture chamber, we found ourselves in a maze of hanging cob webs. I pressed myself as close to Jesus as I could, fearful of what I would encounter next.

Therefore, since we have a great high priest who has gone through the heavens, Jesus the Son of God, let us hold firmly to the faith we profess (Hebrews 4:14).

Satan's Hate Filled Factory

Leaving the murky darkness of Satan's garden, I stepped through a hallway covered in cobwebs onto a landing which overlooked a huge, factory-like room. There were stairs descending down into this ominous place that was filled with a familiar darkness. Sitting down upon the damp landing, I began pulling the sticky, grey cobwebs off myself. At the same time, I tried to comprehend what I was observing.

Demons ruled in this noisy, busy place. They did not use humans to control the prisoners here. From the landing above, I could see large whips in their hands. These whips were made of long, vicious snakes. The fierce snakes appeared to be part of the demon's hands who lashed the prisoners with these living whips. Not only did the snakes whip the bodies of the people they hit, but they sunk their long fangs into them as well. Their bites contained venom that made the prisoners resemble the demons who whipped them. The more they were whipped, the more hate-filled they became.

I assumed that this was the way Satan's chosen humans were prepared to serve as assistance to his demons. Though the humans did not assist the demons in abusing their fellow prisoners in this eerie factory, they were used like slaves. Looking into the damp darkness below, I watched as people, threatened and whipped into submission, pushed dull, black metal carts along a dingy, metal track. Grudgingly they filled the dirty carts with the bones of their comrades.

I could bear no more. Leaving Jesus on the landing, I left the spirit realm and returned to enjoy the loving surroundings of my home and family.

CHAPTER FOUR

Revisiting the Place of Torture

Be self-controlled and alert. Your enemy the devil prowls around like a roaring lion looking for someone to devour. Resist him, standing firm in the faith... (1 Peter 5:8-9).

Just a few days after my sudden retreat from hell, while listening to the Lord in my time alone with Him, He beckon me; "My daughter, I know this is hard for you to see, and I would not ask it of you if it were not imperative. So few believe hell exists, and those who do have no understanding of its reality. It must become very real to you, so you can convey that reality to My children."

Once more I found myself on the dusty, dark platform overlooking the curving staircase into Satan's factory. I heard terrible, piercing screams as my eyes accustomed themselves to the darkness in this large, black pit.

Jesus called, "Follow Me, daughter. What I have to show you must be seen from within the pit."

Carefully I followed Jesus down the metal staircase to the odorous ground level of this factory. Again I saw the demons whipping their victims with the snakes attached to their hands. These people wanted to strike back at the demons, but fear of their captors kept them from retaliating. The hatred and rage in this place was like nothing I had ever witnessed on the earth. I knew that the hatred these demons were injecting their prisoners with through the snake's venom would be controlled by Satan and used to torture other prisoners.

To my utter dismay, I realized that the body parts these people collected and placed in large, metal bins were still alive. If the bones were dead it would have been bearable to watch, but I saw life in the bones. These bones felt the pain and knew that a worse fate was theirs. The terrifying cries I heard were coming from the bins filled with these bones.

The humans pushed the carts filled with the bones along tracks through underground tunnels. The scene was grotesque: Carts filled with bones from which emanated piercing screams and loud moans, while enormous, intimidating demons whipped and cursed those pushing the carts. Snakes were flying through the putrid air, held by the demons controlling them. Their months hung open dripping with the blood of their victims, as they eagerly waited to latch onto their next hostage.

With Jesus' arm around my shoulder, He told me that we had to follow the demonic procession down the tunnel of hatred. It was necessary for me to see where they were going.

As we walked after them He explained: "Satan uses the same devices on the earth as he uses here in hell. He inflicts his victims with hatred. He uses this hatred to control them and to eventually destroy them completely. The venom of hatred is poisonous. Love found in Me is the only antidote for it. As love is the atmosphere of My kingdom, hatred is the atmosphere of Satan's. Wherever you find hatred working, know that Satan or his demons are behind it. It is just as true that whenever you see heartfelt selfless love being expressed; know that I am the author of it."

The Mysterious Cobwebs Explained

While walking through this musty, putrid tunnel, I noticed the same cobwebs that hung at its entrance were hanging from the ceiling and walls here as well. I did not want them to touch me, so I came as close to Jesus as I could. Curiously I asked Jesus what these cobwebs represented.

Answering my question He replied: "The breath of the demons is so filled with hatred; it becomes a web and is used to trap many. Those you see in this place were trapped by the webs of hatred when they lived on the earth. Hatred was the tool the enemy used to control their lives and bring them to hell. Much like a spider's web traps its victim and immobilizes it until the spider comes to kill it, so too, the web of hatred that Satan spins paralyzes his victims until they are his. This is why I have taught My children to love all, even their enemies. Love alone can keep My people out of the webs of hatred. The love everyone needs to stay free is found only in Me. As you saw hatred coming out of the demon snakes and filling their victims with their venom, so too, My love can fill My friends as they encounter Me.

"I am glad you asked Me about the cobwebs," He continued. "They look incidental when you first encounter them, but in reality these webs are very significant. Without these webs of hatred, Satan would have no victims in this part of hell. You were wise to sit and pull the webs off your body before you continued on your journey with Me though this pit. You were also wise to stay close to Me, so these webs would not touch you. Hatred can easily attach itself to anyone who comes near it. When it touches you, it is important that you stop everything and cleanse yourself of it, just as you did when you sat on the landing and pulled the webs off yourself. Repentance and staying close to Me keeps you free of the webs of hatred that Satan spins to trap you."

Avoiding the Strategic Traps of Hatred

Curiosity began to overtake me as I peered into the darkness. I wondered what I would see next. The Lord knew exactly what I was thinking. He told me not to even try to guess what I would encounter next, because no one could imagine the degree of evil that abides in this place. Cautiously I placed my hand more tightly in Jesus' and walked forward dreading what would appear before me.

Tenderly the Lord reminded me to keep my attention fixed on Him as we progressed down the long dismal tunnel; "What you will see will upset you too much if you don't stay close to Me and see it through Me. Never walk alone. Keep your gaze fixed on Me, and I will keep you in perfect peace, even in this place of deep darkness and despair."

Drawing very close to Jesus, so near that His garments enfolded about me, we walked as one through this filthy, black, cobweb infested tunnel. Through the intense darkness I could hear loud clanging sounds and see a faint light ahead. Interrupting my absorption with the darkness, the repetitive sounds and the dim light in the distance, the Lord pointed out a huge, black spider that seemed unaware of our presence. The spider was so shiny it looked wet, which added all the more to its venomous appearance. Undeterred by anything around it, this demon spider quickly climbed the wall beside us, grabbed onto a sticky web and began repairing it. As it worked on this web, I knew instinctively that it was injecting more hatred into the fibers that made up this strategic trap. It was rebuilding a trap of hatred for more unsuspecting victims. A hideous laugh erupted from the delighted spider, as the web increased in size and power.

Jesus explained: "Hatred contains the venom of the enemy and is a deadly trap to all who entertain it in their thoughts. The venom it produces poisons the minds and the hearts of its victims. Hatred is one of the deadliest traps the enemy uses. It delights the demons who manufacture these webs of hatred, because they know how effective they can be in destroying lives. Families are massacred by hatred. Wars erupt and entire towns are leveled in the nations where this web of hatred is allowed to grow. Suffering, death and more hatred are the by-products of Satan's webs of destruction. No one can escape these hideous traps without My help. True love alone can extricate people from these devious webs."

I thought of the times I entertained angry thoughts. How happy I was that the Lord had convicted me quickly so that I did not fall into the trap of hatred the enemy was spinning for me. How many times people had mistreated me and instead of immediately praying for them, in the secret place in my heart, I wished them harm. Each and every time, My Lord was faithful to convict me and lead me to repent. Again and again, He led me to the places in Scripture that taught about forgiveness and loving those who hurt me. He never let me fall so deeply into the trap of hatred that I was unable to get out. Understanding the full impact of the effectiveness of the trap of hatred I thought, "There, but for the grace of God, go I."

Interrupting my introspective thoughts and reading my mind as well Jesus said, "Daughter, I know that you are curious to find out what that clanging noise is coming from the other side of the tunnel. Come, I will show you; remember to stay close to Me."

On our journey out of the tunnel He taught me: "These webs can be avoided while you live on the earth. All that is necessary to keep yourself free of them is found in Me. First love Me with all your heart, then I will give you the love you need for everyone else. Apart from Me it is truly impossible to love freely and purely, but with and through Me, nothing is impossible. Come, My friend, I have much to show you today."

I can do everything through him who gives me strength (Philippians 3:13).

The Chamber of Despair

He has sent me to bind up the brokenhearted, to proclaim freedom for the captives and release from darkness for the prisoners,...to bestow on them a crown of beauty instead of ashes, the oil of gladness instead of mourning, and a garment of praise instead of a spirit of despair (Isaiah 61:1,3).

Fear began to grip me. I wasn't so sure that I wanted to know what was going on outside this dismal tunnel. Because the Lord kept walking, I had no choice but to follow Him and see what He was going to show me in the next chamber of hell.

The clanging noise grew louder and more ominous as we walked forward. It sounded like a sledge hammer hitting large, iron chains. Suddenly an immense, black bat flew in front of us. Jesus was not bothered by it.

He just continued to walk forward instructing me: "Let nothing unexpected frighten you, My child. Though things come at us out of nowhere, nothing surprises Me. That is why it is so important to stay close to Me. I know every devise of the enemy, and I can prepare you for what's coming."

I realized that, as we were walking, all I was thinking about was the loud, clanging noise I heard in the distance. This sound had so captured my attention; I was not prepared for the sudden appearances of the demon spider or the large, black bat. I put my hand in Jesus' strong, steady hand and drew in closer to Him, deciding it was better to watch Him than to keep my attention fixed on the loud, repetitive noise I was so captivated by. Instantly I knew that Jesus was pleased that He was becoming more important to me than this disgusting place was.

Smiling at me He said: "This is the secret of victory over evil. Keep your eyes and attention fixed on Me, and I will see you safely through every trial you encounter. If you become immersed in your problems, you keep Me from protecting and helping you. There is much I want to teach you, but I can only do it if you remain close and connected to My heart."

The Clanging Noise Unveiled

Suddenly I found myself at the edge of a steep cliff. If I hadn't been so close to Jesus, I would not have seen it and would have stepped off into the pit below. Straining my eyes I tried to see where I was, but the Lord reminded me to keep looking at Him and not to stare curiously into the darkness.

As I gazed directly at Him, I saw a large clock suspended high over the pit that loomed ahead of us. Every time the clock ticked it made the loud, clanging sound I had heard while walking through the dark, damp tunnel.

Jesus explained: "Don't try to look at the clock directly; look at it through Me, and I will show you its reality. If you try to see this place outside of Me, you will be deceived and frightened."

It seemed strange to look at evil through the Lord, but I knew I must obey His instructions. The Lord is so beautiful and full of love. Gazing at Him made me feel as if, for an instant, I was in heaven and not in hell. His love was overwhelming me even in this terrible place. I know He was teaching me how to have peace and feel His loving presence even in the midst of the most awful circumstances. I could see Jesus. He appeared to be almost transparent, and through the Lord, I could see the enormous clock loudly ticking in the distant darkness behind Him.

"You have captured the secret of peace in the storm," He encouraged me. "Never forget that I am always with you. No matter what befalls you, I am there, and you can look at the situation through Me." The clanging was not so loud anymore nor the darkness so deep.

The Lord began to show me the horrors His enemy had made for His children in this smoldering pit. In the past, the Lord taught me that heaven is filled with life; there is no death there. Now He showed me that in hell there is no life.

The clock was a torturous reminder to all those abiding in this place that time never ended here. On and on it clanged, one minute after another, never letting anyone forget that they were there forever. Every clang from the clock seemed to shout, "Death, death, death, you are forever dead!"

Tormented by Despair

A putrid, arid smoke ascended out of the dark pit. Despair was the actual ingredient that made up this foggy smoke. Instinctively I knew that this was a chamber in hell where Satan and his demons concentrated their efforts on torturing the minds of those who died and were thrown into this expansive pit.

Jesus counseled: "My presence makes all this bearable, My daughter. Those that are sent here suffer the worse fate of all, being separated from Me for all eternity. They are doomed to never feel loved or accepted. Loneliness dwells in the heart of all assigned to hell. I am love incarnate. Without My presence, there is no love, no kindness, no gentleness and no acceptance. In this chamber, you will see and feel the absence of all that is good. You must look at what I am going to show you through Me, so the despair that fills this chamber won't affect you."

Obediently, while gazing at my Friend, I once again saw the ominous clock that hung over this large, threatening pit. With every clang I could hear demons chanting refrains to demoralize the victims that dwelt here. Loud cries of anguish and despair rose in the deep darkness, just like smoke rises from a fire.

"Alone, alone, forever you will be alone. Unloved, unloved, forever you will be unloved. Separated, separated from all who cared for you. Forever, forever, forever; you are forever separated and alone. Never will you see beauty; never will you hear loving kind words, never, never. Forever sorrowful, forever lost, forever lonely:" were some of the words I heard the demons who ruled this chamber chanting in sync with the clanging clock.

The harder the victims of this torment cried, the louder the demons laughed and chanted. As the people cried in despair, demons stood over them and called out the names of people who had loved them and tried to help them in their lives on earth. These demons would not let the people forget how many times they denied God's help, as He extended it to them through His people. They were not allowed to forget their failings, and they were constantly reminded that they were forever forgotten.

Feeling His Pain

Stopping to weep and hide in Jesus' arms He told me, "My child, do you understand why I lived and died so that none would have to come to this place?"

I could not stop crying. As I pressed close to Jesus and listened to His sorrowful words, I could feel the pain in His heart for those He loved that were suffering so badly, needlessly; "If they had listened to My words of warning and allowed Me to help them, they could have escaped this second death."

Once again the Lord warned me: "Don't try to look around here. Keep your eyes fixed on Me. I will show you only what you need to know to help My children. If you saw all that was here, you could not bear it."

Even though I did not look around, I could feel the utter despair of those living here. There was no silence, no rest from the continuous chanting and reminders of things they wanted to forget. When a demon grew tired of chanting, another came and gleefully took over torturing the poor prisoners.

Utter darkness filled this place that reeked of despair. Tenderly the Lord spoke to me as I wept uncontrollably:

"Thank you for allowing Me to show you this chamber in hell. It is one that fills Me with the most grief. That is why it is so necessary for you to experience it. I need you to trumpet My warning to My children. No one could imagine the degree of evil that fills Satan and his army. It is time to unmask his schemes. I must do all that I can to save My children from this fate. Fear will fill many as they read these words, because they have already heard the sounds of these chanting demons. If they are to escape this torment, they must turn from their sin to Me. I am the Savior of all; none are exempt from My help.

"There are many who live on the earth being tormented by demons. Their minds are held captive by these spirits. Many people believe that hell is on the earth, because Satan does rule over many lives. Though the torment is real, there is an escape from it while they are still on the earth. I am the way of escape. All who cry out to Me can be set free from these tactics of the enemy. No, daughter, hell is not on the earth. Hell is a real place, and once someone is dragged there, it is forever. There is no way of escape out of hell.

"The earth is the Lord's and the fullness thereof! Satan knows the earth belongs to Me, but he is a thief and a liar. He prowls about the earth like a roaring lion seeking who he may devour. His devices are many, but all who turn from him to Me can be protected and find heaven on earth.

"Just like you have seen, those who allow demons to control their lives and thoughts are experiencing a little bit of hell, so too, those who dwell with Me can feel some of the wonders of heaven. Heaven is real and so is hell, but depending on man's choices, you can have a prelude of either while living on the earth. Peace that flows like a river can fill My children's minds, or anxiety, despair and evil surmising can rule their thoughts. What the enemy does in his kingdom, he tries to duplicate on the earth.

"People are not without My help and influence on the earth, because the earth belongs to Me. Once My children become Mine, I have more power to help them resist the enemy. He is a deceiver, but I am truth. My truth will expose every lie he speaks to My people.

Once My truth is heard, the enemy has no power to destroy the lives of My children with his tormenting lies. All this is possible until death comes. I am the Savior of the world, not of those abiding in hell forever. It is never too late to turn to Me before death."

We stepped back away from the black, stench filled pit. I noticed the only light that was present in this place shone from Jesus. As we backed away suffering souls noticed the darkness increasing. They screamed for Jesus to save them, as they realized He was there and saw Him standing at the crest of the pit they were in. Multitudes screamed, yelled His name and reached their arms up to Him, all in vain. I looked at Jesus. Tears streamed down His face. Then I knew it was harder for Him to visit hell than it was for me. These were His children once, but now they belonged to Satan by their choice. No matter how they protested that they hated Satan and wanted another chance to belong to Jesus, it was too late.

I wept, but this time I was comforting Jesus as best I could. With tremendous sadness in His voice, He immediately responded to my overtures of sympathy.

He whispered: "I never forget their pain. When I am not here with you, My daughter, I see them. They are never out of My sight. My pain that you feel is constant. I suffered and died so that they did not have to, but it was to no avail for these. That is why I have brought you here. You must know My heart, so you can reveal it to My people. Daily hell receives more and more of My children. I hear their cries, but I cannot help them anymore. It is too late for them, but it is no too late for the living. Trumpet My warnings fearlessly, and many will escape this pit. I will help you, My daughter."

He continued, "I know it is hard for you to come here with Me. Put your hand in Mine, and I will strengthen and comfort you, dear one."

"It's your pain I feel," I cried to Jesus. "It's your pain that is unbearable, Jesus."

Immediately and emphatically He replied: "The world must know how deep My grief is for those who live here. Many believe I delight in punishing My children by sending them to hell. I do not send them here! They are not Mine. They belong to Satan."

I wanted to hurry out of this place, because I could still hear people yelling to Jesus for help while the clock clanged and the demons chanted their fate. A great desire welled up in me to make Jesus happy. I felt so badly for Him; I wanted to do anything I could to please Him. His suffering was so great for these souls. I knew it was greater than the suffering He endured on Calvary.

"Use my life to save souls," I pleaded. "Take my life, Jesus, and use it to save souls."

Sadly I thought of people I knew who were not following Jesus. Demons influenced them through: hatred, sexual immorality, drug and alcohol addictions or complete indifference to the Lord. I felt His love for them and began to pray for each one to turn to Jesus for help.

After leaving the realm of the spirit, a deep, penetrating sorrow filled me and lasted for days. The sadness that I experienced when I watched Jesus, as He painfully showed me His heart for the lost, was unlike any sorrow I had ever felt. Though I sat in His presence every day; many weeks passed by before He brought me back in the spirit realm to visit another region in hell. I knew He was allowing me the time I needed to recover from the deep grief I felt when I witnessed His tremendous suffering.

We are hard pressed on every side, but not crushed; perplexed, but not in despair; persecuted, but not abandoned; struck down, but not destroyed (2 Corinthians 4:8-9).

CHAPTER FIVE

Doom

You are my lamp, O Lord; the Lord turns my darkness into light (2 Samuel 22: 29).

One very quiet morning Jesus appeared to me enshrouded in great waves of love and peace. The long dreaded day to revisit hell was here. His gentle voice reminded me of His previous instructions.

"Remember," He explained, "whenever I take you to this place of utter darkness and despair, keep your attention on Me. Don't try to observe what is going on unless you look through Me to see what I have to show you."

My Lord continued to instruct me: "You are being brought here by the wings of My Spirit, so when you return to My people, you can warn them of the things that I show you. My friend, I know that it is very difficult for you to come to this place with Me, but it is necessary for the well-being of My children. They need to be warned and told of the horrors of this place."

"Come walk with Me into the darkness," He beckoned, while embracing me with His strong but gentle arm. "I will be your light, so don't be afraid. Stay close to Me, and nothing will be able to touch you."

Suddenly the darkness enveloped us like a black, thick cloud. Through this oppressive darkness I caught a glimpse of large, flying insects. These bugs were like nothing I had ever seen before here or on the earth, though they did seem to resemble the black spiders I had come upon in another chamber of hell. Looking at these flying creatures through Jesus, they became clearer and less frightening. Embraced by His strong loving arm, an overwhelming sadness filled me, because the closer I drew near to Jesus, the more I felt His grief.

"These insects are ambassadors of death and doom," He said very sadly. "Though you can see them clearly here in hell, on the earth they fly about invisible and undetected."

While observing these miniature vultures, I thought of the beautiful butterflies and dragon flies that had so delighted me on the earth. God's creatures reflected His beauty, but Satan's reflected His evil character. They were not colorful or beautiful in any way but were dark, ugly colors and had treacherous, venomous features. Discolored and decaying fangs protruded from their mouths. Their eyes darted about madly in a wild frenzy. Everything about their movements appeared erratic and out of control. As they flew maliciously about me, I quickly tucked in very close to Jesus. Seeing these ferocious, flying demons made me think that being in the darkness was better than being able to see them through the light emanating from Jesus.

Finding a Hiding Place in Him

Warning me He said: "Child, many people feel like you do. They think that what they don't see or know won't hurt them. Like an ostrich hiding its head, so many of My children remain in the darkness rather than coming to Me to receive the light of My truth. Being in the darkness does not cause evil to disappear. Seeing the truth arms you with wisdom to avoid the danger that lurks in the darkness. Hide in Me, not from evil. When you hide in Me and I am truly your hiding place, then no fear will be found in you. When you hide from evil and remain in the darkness, fear will capture your heart. This is not the way of peace and safety. Don't desire the darkness of deception, but come into the light of My presence. Trust Me to show you all you must observe for your benefit and for the good of others."

Jesus' compassionate instruction led me to understand that I was beginning to think in a way that would be a danger to me. Hiding in the darkness from these demon insects was not going to make them go away. Staying hidden in the light of Jesus was going to give me the peace and the wisdom I needed to deal with them.

Confirming my thoughts the Lord explained: "They cannot touch you as long as you keep out of the darkness and stay in the light of My presence. The thought you had to hide in the darkness, so you wouldn't have to see them, was a trick they were trying to use to coax you away from Me. These demons are schemers. They use darkness and deception to trap their victims."

Listening intently to My Friend and Companion, my peace was restored, and I was able to look more closely at what was going on in this ominously, dismal place.

The Injectors of Lies

These flying creatures had sharp claws that descended from underneath them. Unlike the smaller insects on the earth that sting their victims with small stingers, these dark ugly insects used their claws to inject their victims with doom and eventual death. They were capable of landing on the bodies of people and piercing them with their hook like claws. Once they got their claws into a person, there appeared to be no way of escape for the victim. Their function was to inject, through these menacing claws: depression, hopelessness and despair, all rooted in gross deception. They were masters of trickery. Eyes darting feverishly about armed them with the information they needed to exaggerate, manipulate and deceive their victims. Masterful lies were being injected into all they landed on.

Of all the vast number of demonic creatures in hell that I had seen, this was the largest group. There were not very many of them flying in hell because most of them were busy on the earth destroying lives by injecting people with the venom of lies. Those demon insects that were here with us in hell were returning to observe and enjoy their 'victories'. Souls who had been killed as a result of their lies were being wildly celebrated, as they fell into the pit prepared for them.

I heard their jubilant, vicious laughter and squeals of demonic delight, as victims of suicide arrived in this place called Doom. Instead of turning to Jesus for help, many were tricked into overdosing with drugs and alcohol; others were deluded into taking their own lives violently.

"I want to show you their wings, My friend." Jesus said. The wings of these terrible demons had short, sharp, black hairs emanating from underneath the entire wing. These hairs were sticky like fly-paper. As we use fly-paper to trap flying insects on the earth, these demons use their sticky wings to trap people.

"No one is exempt from their traps!" Jesus declared sadly: "Children are especially targeted by them. If they can get close enough to land upon their victim's head or shoulders, they immediately wrap their wings around their faces, so that their eyes are blinded to the truth. All the time they ride upon their victims, they are injecting them with hatred birthed in the lies that have pierced them. Because their eyes are completely closed to the truth, hatred fills them for everyone, including themselves. These demons work in conjunction with others to destroy their victims. This group of demons is especially prideful and likes to take all the credit when someone succumbs to their treachery. When one of My children commit suicide or kills others, they count it as a personal victory."

Taking a step forward the Lord continued: "They leave the task of tormenting these souls, after they are thrown into the fiery pit to other demons, because they believe their task on the earth is too important to leave anyone else to do it. That is why you see them fly in and out of this place so quickly. But for a short visit to observe the final demise of their victim, they spend most of their time ravaging the earth with their venomous lies."

The Way of Escape Explained

As quickly as we had arrived to observe this place in hell that was filled with doom, we returned to a pleasant place in the spirit realm where my trusted Companion continued to help me more fully understand what my spiritual eyes had seen.

"Lord," I asked, "how does anyone escape from these deadly, invisible demon insects?"

"There is no way of escape except through Me," He responded. "That is why I have told My children that I am the way, the truth and the life. Just as I told you to stay close to Me and not to hide in the darkness, that is the same message My people need to know to avoid these injectors of lies. I am the answer. It is easy to find Me, for I will be found by all who seek after Me. While you were in this place of darkness and doom, no insect came near you because I covered you. If I had not opened your eyes to see them, you would not have been aware of their presence. As My people walk in My midst, they will be sheltered and hidden. Never again will they be attacked by these creatures."

After receiving this shocking revelation of these insidious insects from hell, I sat alone with the Lord and was deeply comforted by His loving presence. I remembered the terrible time, years before I had allowed Jesus to be the Lord of my life, when I walked in despair. It was clear to me now that I had fallen victim to one of these creatures. During this dark time in my life, I had grown to hate myself. Because of this self-hatred, I was convinced that my family would have been better off without me. Doom was opening its door to receive me.

But for the wonderful grace of God, I would have succumbed to the trickery of the enemy. During this time of great suffering, Jesus appeared in my life, and He did change the darkness into light. He rescued me from all the lies I truly believed about myself, healed me of the epilepsy that was fueling the overwhelming self-hatred and turned all my sorrows into joy. As I walked with Him and learned His ways, I grew to love and accept myself. Through the past thirty eight years, since He healed me of epilepsy and set me free, the darkness of depression has been kept far from me by the light of His love and His truth. His word is true. He is the way, the truth and the life. Without Him, I would have no life, no truth and no love.

Jesus answered, "I am the way and the truth and the life. No one comes to the Father except through me" (John 14:6).

CHAPTER SIX

The Place of Intolerance

And we urge you, brothers, warn those who are idle, encourage the timid, help the weak, be patient with everyone. Make sure that nobody pays back wrong for wrong, but always be kind to each other and to everyone else (1 Thessalonians 5:14-15).

Suddenly birds were darting all about me. They flew at me and barely missed hitting my head as I ducked away from them. Once again My Friend brought me to the place I had grown to dread. We were walking up a grey, very rocky mountain in the spirit realm when the demon-like birds came at me. Instinctively I knew they were trying to sting me like a bee would and inject venom into my arms. Overtaken by fear, my heart pounding rapidly within my chest, I ran and hid in the folds of Jesus' garment. Peering out from my place of safety, I cried out to Jesus and asked Him what these creatures were.

"Come, do not let them influence you or frighten you," He responded quite calmly. "I have much to show you; your mind needs to be free of all fear so that you can hear Me clearly." Instantly my peace was restored.

The birds continued to swoop down at me, but Jesus was keeping me safe. Encouraging me He said, "As long as you stay close to Me, they can't touch you."

Encountering a Tragic Sight

We walked over to the top of a cliff. Even though we were walking on a rather high elevation, it was dismal and murky here. Unrelenting birds continued flying in all directions about us as we approached the top of the cliff.

The Lord bent down and whispered in my ear: "Don't be afraid. Nothing can hurt or harm you in this place because I cover you. Look through Me as I've taught you in the past, and you will not be troubled by what you see."

Once again as I concentrated on Jesus beside me, the panic left and a great feeling of love and well-being engulfed me. Through Jesus I could see prisoners chained together, clothed in dirty rags, filled with sadness, walking down the side of the cliff we were overlooking. Grotesque creatures snarled and gnashed their teeth at them and frequently whipped the pitiful prisoners, as they forced them to advance down the steep incline toward the bottom of the pit. They knew there was no chance of an escape. A quiet resignation filled each prisoner. What could they have done to cause such cruel and unjust treatment? Completely captivated by this grisly scene, Jesus reminded me to look at it through Him.

These poor tragic figures had no shoes on their feet, and they were stumbling over sharp, jagged rocks. It appeared that they were being made to walk down the steepest and roughest part of the hill. The more terrified and hurt they were, the more it delighted their cruel captors.

As soon as someone lost their balance and fell into the person ahead of them, whom they were chained to, a terrible scene evolved: Cursing and vile screams poured out of the mouth of the person who was pushed and bumped into. There was no mercy or help extended here in this awful place. Rage and anger poured out of the victims along with a terrible hopelessness. Viciously pulling the chain that attached them to the fallen prisoner, the angered soul inflicted so much pain on their collapsed comrade; it caused them to bleed and to cry out in agony.

This brutal response so delighted the demon guards that they joined in on the attack and whipped the stumbling victim. Everyone in this hellish chain gang screamed at him until he got up on his blood drenched feet. Then a dreadful calm ensued as they continued their trudge down the bleak, rocky mountain. Peering into the murky darkness, I watched in amazement as the very one who had responded so viciously to his fallen comrade came crashing down onto the stony ground. Everyone, including the soul he had so brutally victimized, began yelling and pulling on his chains until he rose back to a standing position.

No one helped anyone else here. They just walked down this crooked winding path that appeared to have no end in sight. On and on they went, aimlessly repeating the same riot-like scenario over and over again. Fueled by the rage and anger inflicted on them by the whips of the zealous demon guards, they were continuously pushing, yelling, screaming and pulling one another in a state of hopeless despair.

Accustomed to the darkness, my eyes beheld the enormity of the suffering this mountain held for its many captives. I saw numerous groups of chained prisoners walking barefoot in hopeless misery on their endless journey through a maze of different paths that were scattered up and down its sides. Instinctively I knew many of these prisoners had been walking throughout the walls of this descending pit for many years, even centuries.

The Poisonous Venom of Hatred

"What could these souls have done that would have caused them to be imprisoned in this torturous place?" I asked the Lord once again.

Using the story in Scripture of the Good Samaritan as an example He answered me somberly: "Remember the birds that flew so close to you and tried to inject you with their venom, much like a bee stings its victim? These demon birds fly all over the earth seeking out souls to imprison in this pit of despair and endless futility. Hate is what they try to inject in their victims, the very same hated you saw the prisoners display towards one another. Impatience and intolerance are the open doors that allow these birds to land on people and fill them with venomous hatred. Impatience with weakness, intolerance for those who stumble and fall gives them easy access. As you drew close to Me, you were safe from their attacks. The love that is found only in My heart has patience and tolerance for your falling fellow man.

"Weakness in one's brother or sister can engender resentment so hostile; it relishes the pain the fallen one is enduring. In My Word I warn My children not to rejoice when they see someone suffer for their sins. This is why. It is the character of Satan and his demons to rejoice over the demise of another apparently weaker one. That is not My heart nor My character to rejoice over a fallen one's pain. I am He that comes and lifts up the oppressed.

"In the story of the Good Samaritan, I demonstrated the love and care I show for all who have fallen by the side of the road in their life. It is My tender heart and helping hand that reaches out and lifts the disgraced, even if their own actions caused their demise. I am merciful and patient, always showing compassion and tolerance for the weak and the lowly ones.

"Do not imitate the actions of those who ridicule the weak or criticize and condemn them, but rather, be like Me. Follow in My footsteps, and you will avoid the pitfalls that lead to this place of intolerance.

"When you see or hear of a situation where someone has committed a great crime, come to Me. Just as you came to Me to avoid the birds, come to Me so that you will see that person through Me. I will show you how I see them and allow you to feel My compassion and love for them. The Good Samaritan gave careful instruction and the money needed to the caretaker he appointed to nurse the fallen victim back to health. It is through Me that you will find the resources and the love that you need to help the wounded amongst you. I am the source. If you don't come to Me and draw from My heart, you will fall victim to the spirit of intolerance. Impatience with the weakness of others will fuel your intolerance and bring about your demise if you don't draw close to Me. Independence from Me is not the way to the path of life."

Leaving the spirit realm and returning to the peaceful atmosphere of my home, I began to ponder what I had just seen. The world around me was filled with intolerance: the war in Iraq, the hatred of terrorists, the daily dose of murders and robberies on the news, the politicians condemning one another, on and on. I saw how many times I had embraced an attitude of intolerance and impatience. After my visit to The Place of Intolerance, I was determined that I would see the headlines in the news from a different perspective. Anger would not so easily find a resting place in my heart when I heard terrible stories of injustice. Over and over, with His help, I would bring the events that concerned me to Jesus. No longer was I just praying for those who had awful things done to them. Now I would pray for the perpetrators, too.

My thoughts began to focus on the times I had suffered personally from injustices and been wounded by those close to me. Now I could see each one through Jesus' eyes and could picture myself lending them a hand to stand by my prayers and thoughtful deeds. From now on I was placing a guard around my heart like Jesus taught me. Intolerance and resentment would no longer creep up on me unawares. Resolute and determined, I left my prayer room promising myself that I would never forget the lessons I had learned from my journey into hell this day. *A fool shows his annoyance at once, but a prudent man overlooks an insult (Proverbs 12: 16).*

CHAPTER SEVEN

The Black Hole

Son of man, I have made you a watchman for the house of Israel; so hear the word I speak and give them warning from me (Ezekiel 3:17)

While waiting on my Lord, quietly absorbed in His loving presence, a vision of a white, flowing veil came before me. As I peered through this translucent, glimmering veil, a bold, large, black hole appeared a short distance away. The depth of the blackness of this cylindrical object caught my attention until I saw the smiling face of my Beloved. My heart soared with excitement. I knew He was taking me into the spirit realm with Him. No matter where we went or what He planned to show me, it didn't concern me as long as He was there. Being in His presence was all I longed for.

"Brace yourself My friend, for what I am going to show you today will impact many," He gently warned me as we walked into the spirit hand-in-hand.

Listening for His words, I was not disappointed as He began to explain what the veil represented: "That veil is all that separates you from walking from the natural realm into the spirit realm. Just the faith the size of a mustard seed separates us. Faith allowed Peter, James and John to walk through this veil on the Mt. of Transfiguration into the realm of My glory. Faith launched them through. Today I have given you that same faith, so you can see much more than I have shown you in the past."

Immediately we were walking on the top of the stone strewn, rocky mountain. It was a place that I was familiar with. This place felt ominous, dark and damp. A grey hew hung over it like fog on a misty morning. Together we walked to the edge of the mountain's cliff. I recognized exactly where we were because this was the mountain that the Lord brought me to on my first visit to the land of deep darkness and horror—hell.

With Jesus beside me, I obediently climbed down the iron rung ladder that was attached to the cobblestone wall below. Fear lurked about me as I descended further and further down the dark passage. My Friend understood exactly how I felt. His reassuring nod showed me that He was pleased that I overcame that trepidation and continued on my journey back to hell.

Reaching the base of the ladder, I stepped down on the familiar stony, wet floor. Immediately I heard cries of pain, intermingled with sobs and loud moans. Instinctively I retreated and reached for the silver colored, steel ladder, but my Lord put His arm around my shoulder and gently led me into the darkness.

Shiny, black demons that resembled enormous spiders ran across our path. It appeared that they were unaware of our presence. Cobwebs of hatred draped the walls. I pressed into the side of my Friend as close as I could get, not wanting anyone or anything in this place to touch me.

With words soaked in love and untold understanding Jesus explained: "I have to show you this today. Trust Me to unveil your eyes and guard your heart. There is no way of escape for those who come here without Me. Fear not; you will never come to dwell in this place, but many have and many will. Because I alone am the way of escape, I alone can keep mankind free from the chains that drag them into hell."

Instruments of Torture

Turning the corner I saw a wall filled with large, heavy, rusty chains. I whispered into my Friends ear, "I wish you brought me to heaven today."

He smiled and led me forward into the room that had, not only chains hanging from its walls, but was lined with instruments of torture as well. Large metal tongs, braces, hammers, saws, ice picks and long steel rods were some of the appliances I recognized. Thousands and thousands of them lined this enormous room. Periodically demons, drooling and snarling with anticipation, ran into this hall, grabbed some chains, or picked out a tool and ran out.

My Lord explained: "These instruments of torture are used here in hell and on the earth. Remember what you see here is real, but invisible to the natural eye. One can only perceive them with their spiritual eyes."

Immediately, as quickly as one snaps his fingers, I saw people walking down a busy city street on the earth. Some had their heads clamped with a metal brace around it. A demon sat on their shoulders tightening the brace while tears and grimaces of pain were seen on the faces of their victims. The demons took great delight in inflicting as much pain as they could. Loud snarls and hideous laughter spewed out of their mouths as they tightened the instrument of torture around their victim's skull. Migraines and severe headaches were the lot of those they afflicted.

Other demons shoved long, rusty spikes down the spines of people walking on this city sidewalk. As they sat on their victims shoulders, they hammered these ominous spikes deeper and deeper into their spines. Pain flew everywhere. I could see pain that looked like lightning bolts shoot down arms and legs as the hammering ensued.

Then I observed homeless men and women. Some were sleeping in alleys while others pushed shopping carts filled with their belongings. Many of them attempted to coax those walking by to give them a handout. Though these people were engaged in various activities and in different places throughout this city, all were wrapped in chains. Some had a large, black ball hooked to the end of their chains which they dragged along behind them.

Looking through the crowd, I noted that many who appeared to be affluent had the same chains wrapped around them, just like the homeless did. Little children danced and skipped about beside their parents; most were free of any torturous instruments. But as I watched them, it was apparent that the chains that ensnared their parents were gradually reaching out towards them. Some had a portion of their father's or mother's chains resting on their shoulders. A few walked along wrapped in chains with the smaller black ball being dragged behind them.

Instantly I was back in the room in hell that was filled with instruments of torture and oppression. When I first entered this hallway and saw what the room beside it held, I thought these tools were used to torture the people in hell.

"No, my friend," Jesus explained, "as I have told you in the past, the enemy delights in bringing hell to the earth. Yes, he and his demonic host do use these instruments to torture those they dragged into hell, but that is only a small part of what they do. If they are given permission, they will always hurt and harm on earth as well as in hell."

Jesus declared: "Those who sin delight him the most. The more they sin, the more he owns them, but sin is not the only way he victimizes My people.

"He uses their words against them," He explained further. "When they say, 'I am going to be just like my alcoholic father, or get cancer like my mother or have mental illness like those in my family,' they are his. He takes every negative word spoken by, or over, My people and uses them against them. That is why you saw some young people wrapped in chains. Just spoken words were all the enemy needed to ensnare them in the same chains that oppressed their parents."

Tools of Deliverance

Continuing to teach me He said: "I came to set the oppressed free. I took all these chains and devices of torture on the cross with Me, so mankind would not have to bear them. My grace is all sufficient. This room should be obsolete–it should be extinct. But, alas, so few accept My gift of freedom, and most don't walk in intimate fellowship with Me. If they did, I could hide them under My wing, as I hide you right here in the center of hell from the powers of the evil one. All should be free and untouchable, but most are not.

"It is imperative that you teach them who I am," He declared emphatically, "and tell all what I have done for them. Teach My people how to walk in liberty and in health. I am the way of escape. I am their strong tower. I am their shield and buckler. No weapon fashioned against them can prosper, but they must be Mine. The enemy cannot have any place in their lives."

Then the Lord showed me what this room should look like. It should have been filled with dust from lack of use. Chains should have fallen off their hooks and lay in piles on the floor. Instruments of torture should find no empty places on the shelves and be stacked all over the room. Disuse should bring such rust and deterioration that the links and bolts should have fallen apart.

Instead the room is in constant use. When a person dies the instruments that were used to torture them are returned to this room. Before long they are picked up by a demon and used on another victim.

My Lord counseled me; "Apply My blood. Use the rod of My authority and set the captives free. Exercise the gifts of My Spirit and many will walk out of their chains."

Dangerous Access Points

The Lord reminded me of the large, black hole that I saw as I peeked through the veil and entered the spirit realm today:

"That hole represents the access point the enemy uses to bring a portion of hell to the earth. This was what I wanted you to learn about and see today. Hell is real, and the enemy does bring his elements of torture to the earth through any access he is provided. He does come to steal, kill and destroy (see John 10:10).

"Words are one access point; those words My people speak over themselves and about others are a deep, black passage that gives the enemy entry. There truly is the power of life and death in the tongue. His henchmen stand guard and are alert. They listen for words that they can grab and use against My children." *The tongue has the power of life and death, and those who love it will eat its fruit (Proverbs 18:21).*

"All occasions of sin are another path the enemy travels on to bring tormenting spirits from hell," my Lord explained. "To be safe My children must avoid sin. By My grace this is possible."

He added: "Another very powerful access point that few recognize is also used. This channel is full of activity bringing tormenting beings to the earth on a continuous basis. When I am denied, when I am slandered, when I am not trusted or believed, demons rejoice. No greater channel to the earth exists. Unbelief keeps My people in bondage to their tormentors after access is granted. When I walked the earth, unbelief kept many in the grip of tormenting spirits. The lack of faith of those I encountered denied Me access. Daughter, tell My people to deny the enemy access to their lives."

Job's Story

Seeing this black chasm and hearing the Lord's admonition reminded me of the story of Job. What a holy man Job was. He loved God and hated sin. One eventful day when the angels came to present themselves before God, Satan came, too. How brash he was–to appear before the Holy One with no apology but in utter contempt and consummate pride. There Satan stood.

In the midst of their conversation, God pointed to his servant Job and said, *"There is no one on earth like him; he is blameless and upright, a man who fears God and shuns evil." (Job 1:8).*

What a stark contrast existed between Satan and Job. How deep Job's love was for God, and how tremendous was Satan's hatred for the Almighty. How humble was the man called Job–totally dependent on his God and grateful to Him for all He did. While the pride of Satan was so enormous, it took on a life of its own. Satan looked jealously at Job and saw the antithesis of all he was. How he hated Job! Job was loved by God and blessed by Him more than any man alive. He was the wealthiest man of his day and lived blessed in every way. Satan salivated at the thought of destroying this man and all he owned.

Filled with scorn, Satan berated God and declared that Job only loved Him because of all God had given him:

"Does Job fear God for nothing?" Satan replied. "Have you not put a hedge around him and his household and every-thing he has? You have blessed the work of his hands, so

*that his flocks and herds are spread throughout the land. But
stretch out your hand and strike everything he has, and he
will surely curse you to your face" (Job 1:9–11).*

It was clear that Job had allowed Satan and his demons no access
to his life. The black hole was blocked. The hedge was shut tight
around him and his. Satan couldn't touch the man who knew he was
loved by God and who wholeheartedly loved Him in return.

When Satan accused Job and God, the Mighty One listened. He
heard the accusation that Job only loved God because of all He had
given him. Satan sneered that if Job lost all he had, he would surely
turn against God. Was Satan implying that God was only loved
because of what He gave and not because of who He was? Was
he telling the Almighty that He was not worthy of true devotion?
God knew Job's heart, and He knew his love was pure. He would
allow Satan access through the black hole, through the dark chasm
connecting hell to the earth, to test Job's love for him. The world
would see so great a love, too. God handed Satan the key to the
hedge that formerly denied the destroyer access to Job's life.

The Hedge

This divinely constructed hedge didn't just protect Job from
Satan's schemes. It also enclosed his household and all he possessed.
Now Satan had the key. The permission was his, which sin did not
grant, that no word curses had permitted, that unbelief had not
allowed entry through. Satan wasted no time. He allowed himself to
be true to his name, the destroyer.

In one day, using his access key, Satan and his henchmen brought
the ravages of hell to the earth. Traveling through that black hole
from hell, his demons rallied the Sabeans to steal all Job's oxen and
donkeys while killing his servants. At the same time, the destroyer
sent fire to consume all Job's sheep and servants. Minutes later, the
Chaldeans were loosed to form three raiding parties and steal all
Job's camels and kill his servants. Satan saved the worst for last.
Death left hell and was sent to Job's son's house. All his children
were enjoying one another's company and were feasting there. A

mighty wind sent from hell swept in from the desert and destroyed the house. All his children were killed instantly. Job's beloved seven sons and three daughters were no more.

> *At this, Job got up and tore his robe and shaved his head. Then he fell to the ground in worship and said: "Naked I came from my mother's womb, and naked I will depart. The Lord gave and the Lord has taken away; may the name of the Lord be praised." In all this, Job did not sin by charging God with wrongdoing (Job 1:20–22).*

Kept Safe by His Blood

From the events of Job's life, we can see the tremendous power the enemy has to destroy our lives, our possessions, our loved ones and our health if we give him access. Just one sin, just one offense against God, gives Satan permission to bring the ravages of hell to bear on us.

For the accuser of our brothers, who accuses them before our God day and night, has been hurled down (Revelation 12:10). His name suits him well—the accuser of the brethren. Nothing delights Satan more than finding flaws in God's children. Once he discovers those sins, then he can justify attacking them.

Truthfully we all have sinned, not just once but many times. Without the power that is in the blood of Jesus, there would be no hope for any of us. Thankfully He *has freed us from our sins by his blood (Revelation 1:6).* Not only has He shed His blood to cover our sins and paid the full price for us to be free from Satan's grip, but He is a consuming fire that burns up all of our sins, so we will be forever protected. *"And I myself will be a wall of fire around it," declares the Lord, "and I will be its glory within."(Zachariah 2:5).*

To access this wall of fire and the sin cleansing power of His blood, we need first and foremost faith in Jesus Christ. Faith in Jesus becomes a wall of protection around our lives, like the wall or hedge that surrounded Job. Could it be that simple? Could just believing in our Savior and receiving the benefits of what He did for us on the cross at Calvary be sufficient to keep us safe from the devil and his schemes?

The answer is, most assuredly, yes. Scripture informs us that if we express faith in Jesus, believing that He truly is the Son of God, we will be saved (see John 3:16). In order to do this, we must acknowledge that He left heaven and came to the earth to die on the cross to pay the price for our sins. For this wonderful gift to apply to our lives, we must repent, or express true sorrow for our sins, which He always forgives, and then begin to follow Him. (See 1 John 1:9.)

Once we make a sincere commitment to be His and invite Him to come and live in our hearts, He will become a wall of fire surrounding our lives. Our pledge to live for Him brings His unfailing promise to love and protect us. Then we can be assured that He will bring us safely home into His kingdom, where we will live forever when we leave this earth.

Renounce Satan and Live Blessed

But just receiving eternal life and His protection is not all Jesus purchased for us. Galatians 3:13 declares that, *Christ redeemed us from the curse of the law by becoming a curse for us*. He made the way for us to live blessed and not under a curse. He died on the cross so we could be free from all curses: the curse of poverty, sickness, premature death, rejection, etc.

For us to receive all of the blessings He so painfully purchased for us, it is important that we not only repent for our sins, which bring curses on our lives, but that we renounce Satan and the sins we have committed. To renounce means to declare to God and to Satan that we give up, or disown, the sin and our relationship with Satan which that sin initiated. Without our knowing it, when we sin we hand the key to the hedge, or the invisible wall, around our lives to Satan and his henchmen and grant them full access to us and ours. As we humbly come before Jesus, confess our sins, renounce them and the spirits attached to them, we strip the key to our lives out of Satan's hand.

For example, if we renounce stealing from our neighbor, we are in fact telling Satan we want nothing to do with him and take back the authority we gave him over our lives when we sinned by stealing. After praying that simple prayer, the enemy no longer has permission to come and steal from us because we stole from others. As we totally surrender our lives to Jesus, we are giving the Lord the key to the invisible hedge that surrounds our lives. Once we do this, the Lord has our permission to keep us safe and blessed.

I have made it a practice to help many individuals to receive the full freedom that Jesus purchased for them. After they have confessed their sins and turned their lives over to Jesus, I lead them to renounce those things that have brought curses or strongholds in their lives. For example, I ask them to renounce the spirit of bitterness and unforgiveness in the name of Jesus. Then I break every curse the spirit of bitterness (or any other sins they have committed) has brought on their lives and place those curses under the blood of Jesus. I end our prayer session by commanding all the blessings Jesus intends for them to have to come forth: the blessings of a beloved child, the Baptism of the Holy Spirit, all the gifts of the Holy Spirit, health, happiness, restored families, prosperity, etc. ... *how much more will your Father in heaven give the Holy Spirit to those who ask him? (Luke 11:13).*

For all who have truly repented for their sins, renounced Satan and all their sins, put every curse that has come on their lives under His blood, they, too, can live blessed, protected and fulfilled lives. Like Job, those things that were stolen will be restored just by commanding it to be so in the name and authority of Jesus. Job received back double what he had lost after he passed the test he endured. He even received ten more children, and these were far more beautiful and endearing than the ten sons and daughters that Satan had killed.

Jesus made a way, not just for us to be protected and safe; that wasn't good enough for His beloved bride. No, He also provided us access to all that that heaven holds. Just like the enemy brings some of hell through his black access route, Jesus gives us access to what heaven has, too. Once we are free from the curse, Jesus told us we can ask for anything in His name and it will be ours; *"I tell you the truth, my Father will give you whatever you ask in my name" (John 16:23).*

Remember He became a curse, so we could be blessed:

Christ redeemed us from the curse of the law by becoming a curse for us, for it is written: "Cursed is everyone who is hung on a tree." He redeemed us in order that the blessing given to Abraham might come to the Gentiles through Christ Jesus, so that by faith we might receive the promise of the Holy Spirit (Galatians 3:13–14).

CHAPTER EIGHT

Kingdoms Compared

Then I saw a great white throne and him who was seated on it. And I saw the dead, great and small, standing before the throne, and books were opened. If anyone's name was not found written in the book of life, he was thrown into the lake of fire (Revelation 20:11, 12, 15).

A few weeks had passed since my riveting visitations to hell. Then with no warning, the Lord appeared one morning and beckoned me to come with Him. In this divine encounter, He brought me into the spirit realm to revisit both the place I hated and the place I longed to see.

As I peered into the spirit, I saw the top of the mountain where the Lord had led me months earlier. Timidly I walked to the side of the steep cliff and looked into the deafening darkness below. I saw the metal ladder and the wall to which the rungs were connected. Bones, the lively building stones of Satan's world, meshed together to make a horrific wall. I looked up at my Master, questioning Him with my glance.

As always He answered my thoughts; "Yes, My friend, I do want you to descend with Me into hell today."

While descending down the hellish stairwell, I felt the darkness and gloomy dampness envelope me like a musty, black cloak. I could hear the trickling sound of water running below. When I reached the bottom of my descent through the darkness, I saw water barely covering the floor. The bumps were exposed, and all the crevices were filled with the filthy, black water. Hanging onto the steel wrongs, I grimaced in repulsion hoping I would not have to step down on this putrid floor.

"Come, daughter. Do not fear for I will make a way for you. Just follow in My footsteps," my Savior beckoned as He encouraged me to launch out into the new territory He was showing me today.

Gingerly I carefully stepped down fearing that the corpse-like floor would be slippery from the slimy water covering it. After taking the first step, I saw a clear, clean path wherever Jesus stepped. His footprints kept my feet free from the grimy water's grasp. A little part of me felt like Peter when he stepped out of the boat on the raging sea. Peter sank after a few steps, because the fear of sinking captivated his thoughts. Determined not to make the same mistake as Peter did, I held fast to the wonder of watching the water part under my Lord's feet.

A joyous delight filled my heart as I quickly stepped into each footprint. What amazed me the most was that as I stepped in the place where His foot had been, I felt His glory fill my heart. "Lord, how is it possible for me to feel your glory in this terrible place?" I asked.

"If you stay close to Me and follow in My footsteps wherever I lead you, you will always feel My glory," He responded. "No matter what the circumstances surrounding you, if you stay close to Me, you will feel My love and not the hatred of the foe."

I was so engrossed by the wonder of this revelation that I didn't look at my surroundings. My eyes were firmly fixed on His footprints beneath me and His form in front of me.

"No matter where you go in life put this truth into practice," He counseled me. "Keep your eyes fixed on Me and whatever is going on around you won't affect you. Now come and stand beside Me, My friend." As the Lord spoke, He stopped and drew me beside Him.

I moved as close to Him as I could, feeling the warmth of His garments strengthened me. Though I hated this place that He brought me to, I loved Him more. I told Him I was willing to go wherever He led me, and I meant it! I knew no matter what He was going to show me, I was safe standing next to Him. Fear escaped me like steam rising from a pot of boiling water.

Looking around I saw nothing. All was in complete darkness. The only thing I could see was Jesus' form standing so tall and commanding next to me.

He exclaimed, "I am going to open your eyes, so you can see what I want to show you today, My friend!" When He said these words, it felt like the light that was in Him poured through me and out of my eyes. I thought I was going to see a wall, but what I saw was just the opposite. I observed a large land that stretched out before me for as far as I could see.

The Pit-Laden Land

With a deep gasp, I peered through the illumined darkness. Everything was black and lifeless. Death dwelt in this land. Thick, black smoke escaped from large pits that were scattered haphazardly throughout the terrain. Ghastly, black, inhumane creatures climbed out of the pits. Saliva hung from their mouths, while venomous hatred poured out of their fiendish eyes. Some demons walked on two legs, others crawled on four. Escaping from the smoke laden pits were endless screams and heart wrenching moans. It appeared that whenever the screams increased in volume and intensity, the demons responded with sneers that resembled smiles. As I watched this scene, I saw these demonic creatures scale the wall that I had just climbed down and disappear over the ridge.

Hell was a lonely place. Apart from the screams and loud moans, a deafening silence hung over the land like a dense fog on a very dismal night. No one talked. Even the demons I saw were silent, except for occasional growls and snarls. Purpose appeared to inundate their lives. It was clear that they lived to find victims they could torture forever.

Gasping in horror, I saw large animal-like demons appear back at the top of the cliff overlooking hell. This time they were not alone. Each one dragged a human being behind them: Some were slung over their shoulders; others were pulled along by their hair, while many were dragged by their limbs. All the victims were screaming for help, for mercy, for another chance. The demons only laughed and snarled. They treated their victims like trophies.

I clung to Jesus and, as this scene evolved before me, He spoke; "Daughter, what you are observing is happening as we speak. I am not showing you a fantasy or something that might happen in the future. No, My dear, this is a reality, and souls are being brought to hell now!"

Then to my dismay, I saw a demon drag a helpless woman to one of the pits. Frantically she clawed the ground trying to grab hold of something that would help her get away. All her efforts were in vain, because this evil creature was no match for her meager strength. Once the black demon brought his screaming victim to the edge of the pit, it rolled her to the edge and kicked her down into the fiery pit. At that moment, I had to put my hands over my ears to deafen the noise of her piercing screams and the demon's hideous laugh.

I buried my face in the Lord's robe. "Lord, this is too terrible to face," I cried as I clung to Jesus.

I knew that these demons watched and waited for just the right opportunity to kill their victims when they lived on the earth. Those who lived far from God and walked a path of compromise with evil met their demise when Jesus had no right to save them.

I felt Jesus' extreme disappointment and deep heartache. He lived and died so that all could inherit His kingdom, so none would come to this place of endless suffering. The scene before me was not His will, but it was the will of the evil one and his mob of demons.

Walking very slowly, giving me time to muster more courage, the Lord led me to the edge of the smoke laden pit that had swallowed its screaming victims. The closer I got the more the smoke thickened and burned my eyes. Wiping the tears from my eyes, I made myself look into the pit. Through the dense smoke, I could see flames and glowing embers.

The pit was a prison that had no way of escape. It was built that way. The walls were slanted away from the circumference of the central hole at the top so that no one could scale the sides and escape. Some were trying to get out but would only get a few feet high, and they would fall back to the floor of this living furnace. It resembled the shape of a volcano, but the bed of flames was at the base where all the victims suffered relentlessly.

No one sympathized with anyone here. All were absorbed in their own torment. In fact, when one of their co-sufferers tried to scale the wall and failed, it appeared that those who stood by and watched breathed a sigh of relief as they fell. It made no sense. I thought, "Why don't they help one another get out? Perhaps they could come up with a plan that would help some of them scale the slanted walls."

While I watched, I noticed that there were no demons guarding them. These grotesque creatures knew no one would get away. Instead, they spent their time gathering more victims from the earth and dragging them into this pit laden part of hell.

My Friend stood silently beside me as I looked at this horror-filled scene. To watch people suffer and be completely unable to help was a torment we both shared.

The level of suffering was so great that it never abated. There was no resignation, no sighs, just continuous screams and expressions of relentless pain. As I watched, I saw some of the victims scrape their wounds with broken sharp objects that looked like broken pottery. This scene reminded me of the story of Job in Scripture.

As we have discussed in an earlier chapter, Job was a very faithful friend of God. Job suffered terribly at the hands of Satan but remained faithful to God even after losing everything: his ten children, all he owned and his health. After Satan killed his children and stole his possessions, he afflicted him with painful sores all over his body. To relieve the pain to a minute degree, Job scraped the wounds with broken pottery.

This was what I saw when I looked into that pit: people in hell scraping their rotting flesh. When people complain that hell is on earth, they are only seeing a small piece of that picture. Hell is a very real place, but Satan and his henchmen delight in bringing some of the suffering they inflict on their victims in hell to anyone they can reach on the earth. Now I knew that Satan had brought a small portion of hell to the earth and heaped it on the body of God's faithful friend, Job.

So Satan went out from the presence of the Lord and afflicted
Job with painful sores from the soles of his feet to the top

of his head. Then Job took a piece of pottery and scraped himself with it. As he sat among the ashes... (Job 2:7-8).

Job suffered with a heart of acceptance and remained faithful despite his pain.

That was not the attitude of those who endured the pain that the flames afflicted them with here in hell. "Where's God? I thought He was the Savior of the world. I never believed in His power while I lived, and I surely don't now." These were just a few of the remarks I heard them yell with disgust and hatred.

How sorry I felt for them. If they had only met my Lord briefly when they lived on the earth, they would have found out how wrong they were. My Friend could have, and would have, saved them from this eternal world of torment. Just a glimpse of Him, just a touch from His hand, a gentle word spoken to their hearts could have made a world of difference for them. But they would not let Him come close. How sorry I felt for them.

"Daughter, this is why I call you to reach the lost," Jesus whispered. "This is why I propel you into the darkness to bring the light of My presence. It is through My chosen vessels that I am able to reach the lost before it is too late."

The Other Kingdom

Then He encouraged me with these words: "Come with Me, for now I will show you the other side. There are many who have escaped this eternity of suffering, because of the obedient service of those who follow Me and go to those I send them with the message of the Gospel."

To my relief we turned and walked back to the wall. Almost effortlessly I climbed back to the green, grassy embankment overlooking hell. In sheer emotional exhaustion, I collapsed on the ground and wept uncontrollably for those who had no hope in the land beneath us. My Lord comforted me. As He did, I knew that it was I who should be comforting Him. These were His beloved children. He died for them and loved them more than I could ever imagine. Instead He held me close to His heart and let me cry until I could cry no more.

"I won't give up trying to reach those who have never met you, Lord. I will persevere no matter how thick the opposition," I cried. As I sobbed, I told him I would never complain again about how difficult the ministry was.

I thought of the teenage boys I visited two times a week at the local detention facility. Hundreds had met Jesus during our mid-week service. Just a touch from Jesus was all it took, and they were transformed. Hard hearts were softened. Sins were repented for and renounced and wholehearted commitments were made to follow Jesus. Watching the glow on the boys faces as they encountered Him during worship would be my greatest reward. Knowing that they would never experience the horrors of hell would keep me steadfast and devoted to the work I was assigned to accomplish for my King. My job was simple. All I had to do was introduce them to Jesus. He would do the rest.

"Do you feel better, My child? Are you ready to come with Me?" Jesus asked gently. I felt cherished and understood. His compassion filled me with a new-found strength.

While He hugged me, I looked over His shoulder and saw an enormous, gold staircase. Angels, magnificent creatures dressed in glistening, white garments accented with gold, smiled back at me. They stood at the bottom of the majestic staircase and lined the sides of it for as far as I could see into the shimmering, blue heavens above.

VISITS TO HEAVEN

I keep asking that the God of our Lord Jesus Christ, the glorious Father, may give you the Spirit of wisdom and revelation, so that you may know him better. I pray also that the eyes of your heart may be enlightened in order that you may know the hope to which he has called you, the riches of his glorious inheritance in the saints...(Ephesians 1:17-18).

CHAPTER NINE

His World Displayed in all its Wonder

I looked up and there before me was a man dressed in linen, with a belt of the finest gold around his waist. His body was like chrysolite, his face like lightening, his eyes like flaming torches, his arms and legs like the gleam of burnished bronze, and his voice like the sound of a multitude (Daniel 10:5-6).

His presence was better than life. Such joy filled my heart; all I could do was weep with happiness. Looking at the golden staircase rising behind my Lord, we turned and laughed together as we began to climb into the heavenly realm. Each gold step looked like a shiny mirror that reflected the glory of Jesus. The higher I climbed the deeper the intensity of His glory became. I could barely breathe. His presence was breathtakingly magnificent; it radiated from the translucent, glorious staircase.

The angels that lined the stairway were different sizes; all were beautiful, absolutely grandiose. Each of them stood outside the stairs. Those who were enormous stood towards the back and were surrounded by high, wispy clouds in the sky. God's angels were mighty, a force that none could resist, but at the same time, a quiet gentleness poured forth from their smiling faces (see Isaiah 38).

Walking up the angel lined stairs I told Jesus, "I feel safe."

Laughing at my simplicity He said, "Child, that is My desire, to make all who follow Me safe and secure. See these angels that surround you today. I have given them My command to take care of you, not just today but always."

I asked the Lord if He would let me see the faces and the garments of the angels in more detail. In response to my request, He immediately opened my spiritual eyes to see the exquisite details of heavens' hosts. It was as if He held a magnifying glass against their garment. As I looked I saw the intricately woven fabric of the angels' clothing. Gold fibers were woven with crystal-clear strands that looked like diamond threads. The grandeur of their clothing was astounding.

Then I saw the face of an angel very clearly. It was shiny and resembled the color of highly polished bronze, magnificent, like nothing I had ever seen before. The Lord reminded me that their faces constantly reflect the glory of God. I surmised that the angels get sun-tanned from the radiant light that pours forth from God, but in heaven it is healthy!

All the angels were arrayed in different wardrobes; some wore gold, loosely fitted pants; others had white or golden robes tied with glittering gold belts. I was amazed at how different each one was dressed. As I thought this the Lord laughed and said, "My kingdom is not boring! It is truly marvelous and reflects My glory. Look at the splendor that I pour out on the wardrobes of My angels. Can you imagine the opulence that I am going to shower upon those who have never seen Me but still remain faithful to Me?"

The Lord reminded me of this Scripture when I saw the way He showered His love on His angels: *Yet I tell you that not even Solomon in all his splendor was dressed like one of these... How much more will I clothe you? (Matthew 6:29, 30).* I knew the reward He has planned for His friends far outweigh what we could ever imagine. *Then your father, who sees what is done in secret, will reward you (Matthew 6:4).*

With breathtaking awe, I observed how immensely different the angels surrounding this staircase were compared to their counterpart in hell. Love emanated from the angelic beings, along with a deep loyalty and submission to their King, while the demons were filled with hatred and a deep-seated rebellion. One group was as beautiful and as glorious as any could ever imagine. The others were uglier than the most hideous monster one had ever seen depicted by any artist.

The demons didn't resemble anything that lived on the earth. They were black and had scales covering them. Their bodies looked like an animal which had long legs with claws extending from its feet. Some had two legs and two arms, others had four legs. They were shaped like birds that resembled dinosaurs, and their heads had large eyes that were slanted and evil in appearance. Their mouths were oversized and lined with fangs that dripped with slimy saliva. Vapor emanated from their wide nostrils, truly a monstrous site.

The angels reflected the beauty of God, while the demons took on the character of Satan. The more the angels were in the presence of God, the more they took on His likeness: loving, kind, helpful, gracious. I could understand why people fell prostrate at the feet of angels, because they had absorbed so much of His goodness. He alone is worthy to be worshiped (see Daniel 10:4-19).

A Promise Made

As we ascended the golden stairs the Lord stopped and looked in my eyes: "My friend, I have watched as you faithfully served Me. All that you have done has not gone unnoticed, nor will it go unrewarded. I have also watched those who have come alongside you in the ministry. These, too, I will reward. I have observed them obey My promptings and watched as they supported your efforts to reach the lost for My kingdom's sake. Just like Aaron and Hur held up Moses' tired arms, many have raised up your arms when you were languishing. There were those who encouraged you and sent finances to accomplish what I have called you to do. Others stood beside you and labored with you, while many stood in the gap and diligently prayed for you and for those you were sent to. All of these I am going to bless in this season."

Filled with curiosity I asked, "Lord, how will you bless them?"

"My friend," He responded, "I will give them their heart's desires, just as I gave you yours." I laughed when he showed me that one might want a new puppy, while another would not want a dog. Each would get exactly what they most deeply desired!

"All who sowed faithfulness to you," He continued, "and to Me will receive a rich harvest of My faithfulness to them. I do reward those who diligently serve Me!"

From the week the Lord spoke this promise to me, many of those who have helped me with His work have received tremendous blessings: jobs and promotions were received by some; a few were able to easily purchase new homes; others sold property that had been on the market for years; some even sold property that was not up for sale; broken relationships have been restored; physical infirmities have been healed.

Coming to the top of the gold staircase, I stepped on the cloud laden floor and felt the blue sky enveloped me with its warmth. Looking into the distance, I saw what I call the outskirts of heaven: a land of rich foliage, cascading colorful flowers and lush green grass. The path I stepped onto was made of stepping stones. One was a large ruby, another was an emerald and then an opal; even a large flat diamond was there for all to walk on. The colors were rich and breathtakingly stunning to behold. The grass was such a vibrant green; it looked like it was painted by an illustrious artist.

Then I saw a magnificent, ornately carved, gold bridge. It covered a sparkling river that was fed by a splendid waterfall. This gleaming river flowed over large, gold nuggets and rocks; some were the size of boulders. The light that reflected off the golden waterfall shimmered on everything. The lush, green grass sparkled and looked like millions of diamonds had been scattered all over it. With the Lord's arm wrapped around my shoulder, we walked over the bridge.

Never have I wanted to stand and absorb a scene as much as I did at that moment, but my Friend gently coaxed me forward. I felt His enthusiasm. There was something very special He wanted to show me. Leaning on my Beloved, I held fast to all I saw. I never wanted to forget this glorious place. Artistically planted beside the waterfall were colorful flower gardens and heavily laden fruit trees. The dewdrops that danced on each petal and leaf looked like precious gems shimmering in the light.

"Come, My daughter. This is but a prelude of what I want to show you," the Lord explained as we stepped off the elegant country bridge back onto another jewel laden path.

No Christmas light display on the earth could ever compare with the colors and the vibrancy of the lights that reflected off these stones. When God placed the rainbow in the sky, I think he took a little bit of heaven and shared it with us, a prelude of things to come. Even as beautiful as a rainbow is, it is but a shadow of the depths of the colors in heaven.

The further we walked the more brilliant the colors became. Now I understood why my Friend wanted me to keep walking. Standing on the bridge and looking at the majestic scene would have satisfied me until I saw the sight unfolding in front of me. Now it was me pressing forward to see all; ever-increasing glory was what I was experiencing.

My Lord laughed, amused at my delight in His homeland. As we embarked up the path into His kingdom, I heard the melodious chirping of birds. Even the color of parrots and macaws dulled in comparison. So vibrant were the colors of the feathers of these friendly birds, they could be seen no matter where they flew. Brilliant reds, yellows, oranges, blues, violets and magenta's were but a few of the colors I observed.

Some flew close to us, and with a gentle nod of permission from Jesus, a few landed on our shoulders. Nestled close to our necks and faces, we were showered with affection and attention from the Lord's happy greeters. It reminded me of the attention dogs give their masters when they return home. We were greeted with the love of one who longs for its beloved. A soft white dove sat on my shoulder. No claws dug into my skin, but gentle and light were the feet of these sweet birds. With my head resting on the Lord's shoulder, the cooing dove gently nestled near my other cheek. The Lord laughed merrily as birds sat on His arms and shoulders. What a sight!

As we walked forward, I kept glancing back at the waterfall, the bridge and the sparkling floral scene we had just left. I never wanted to forget it. I wanted it etched into my memory forever. Joyfully my Friend declared, "Daughter, do not worry; what I have revealed to you today, you will never forget."

Eyes of Faith Opened

He continued: "I have prepared a beautiful home for My faithful children. No eye has seen, no ear has heard, nor has it ever entered the heart of men what I have in store for them. Daughter, do you see what I have revealed to you today? That is but a glimpse into the delights I have stored up for My friends. I am a good God and a doting father. It brings Me great delight to lavish My children with the glorious riches of My kingdom. To fill your heart with joy brings Me great satisfaction. Even greater is the joy I feel when I see My children turn down the riches of the world for more of My presence. For those who have sincerely sought hard after My nearness, I will withhold no good thing."

Each time I looked back at the waterfall, it appeared larger and clearer. Faith made everything bigger and brighter. The waterfall was enormous and reached high into the golden mountains over-shadowing us, while the river tumbled under the bridge and stretched out into a vast expanse of land. Fruit trees laden with fruit of every kind were being fed by the river. Their leaves never withered, and they never failed to bear fruit (see Psalm 1).

I knew that the Lord was showing me that the greater my faith was in Him and in what He was revealing to me, the clearer I would see into His world. He explained: "The greater your faith is in Me, the greater the miracles I will be able to do through you, for every-thing happens to the degree that you believe. When I healed the blind man, first he saw men that look like trees. Then with another touch and an increase in his faith, he saw clearly (see Mark 8:22-26). You will receive whatever you believe. If you believe that you will receive a small revelation that is what you will get. If you believe that I will show you the glories of My kingdom, then, that is what you will see. Expand your faith; then look and see what I will show you. Believe and receive of My fullness, My friend."

With eyes of faith, I turned around and looked back at the scene intently. Oh, how amazing! Now I could see angels and children gathering fruit from the trees along the river bank. They were laughing and dancing together. Some children were in the trees throwing fruit down into the baskets of those who caught them below. This reminded me of the scene I first encountered on one of my earlier visits to heaven. What I had seen years before was glorious, but today I was able to see so much more and with such clarity and detail; it amazed me.

The river emptied into a beautiful lake where other children and angels swam together. Though great joy filled everyone, I was impressed by something else. Love, exuberant love, poured out of everyone, the children and the angels as well. They looked like they were swimming in a sea of love.

No matter how many times the children squealed, "Look at me dive. Look at how high I can jump. Look at how deep I can swim;" the angels never got tired of responding to those who they were guarding so lovingly. They had an assignment from their King to watch these youngsters, and they did it wholeheartedly.

My heart leapt with joy as I realized that I could have walked by this scene and never seen it, but my eyes of faith were opened by the gentle coaxing of the Holy Spirit: "There is more. Keep looking. Believe and you will see the glory of your God revealed."

God was teaching me a valuable lesson about faith. If we have a little faith, press for more. Believe God for His best. Don't let unbelief limit what God will do for us. We will receive only as much as we believe. Like the father who prayed, "*I do believe; help me overcome my unbelief!" (Mark 9:24)*, we must pray, Lord, I believe. Help my unbelief. Help me believe in all you can do and all that you are.

To my utter amazement, the blue sky turned into a vibrant rainbow. Unbelief had limited my ability to see it as it was, but now it had been removed. I believed and I saw. What a sight! Such a splash of colors hit my eyes, like the hue of the light when it hits a prism and reveals the colors of a rainbow, so brilliant!

The children who had gathered the fruit called out to those who were swimming to come and eat. What a party they had! Pleasant music floated through the land. A rainbow sky embraced everyone. Colorful birds joined in the festivities and ate alongside the children as they held their food out to them. I watched a heavenly picnic. Some of the children ate while others played baseball. Many played tag and hide-and-seek. The harder I looked, the more I saw.

Over the hillside were games and activities supervised by the guardian angels. Soccer, polo with horses, tennis, baseball, volley-ball and hopscotch were just some of the activities they enjoyed. I never saw so many children having so much fun without any chaos or confusion. It looked like a great Olympic festival. When they wanted a break, down the hill they ran and raced each other to the lake. In they ran, seeing who could splash the most and swim the fastest.

The Lord explained: "This is real! This is what goes on in My kingdom. There is fun for all. That is why I prodded you to go fur-ther when we were walking over the golden bridge. I wanted you to go further in the spirit and deepen your faith, so you could see all I wanted to reveal to you today. Each time you looked back, you saw more. With eyes of faith and expectancy, you looked again and again. Each time your eyes were opened to see the truth.

"Don't just catch a glimpse of who I am," He prodded me. "Look deep into My Word, and you will see more and more of Me. You could settle for a quick glance and be satisfied with that, but I have so much more for you. Never be satisfied; always seek after more of Me. That is the secret to receiving My fullness."

Then I saw a boy hit a home run. The ball flew high and far toward us, right into the hands of Jesus. Everyone stopped. They saw Jesus laughing, holding the ball. Instantly they all ran to Him. He stood in the midst of them, and they all sat around Him just gazing into His face and listening for Him to speak. When He spoke each child heard Him talk directly to them. How He did it, I don't know, but each one received a special message at the same time. All were satisfied and delighted by what He said to them. Then He laughed, patted them on their heads, hugged many, picked some up, and kissed others until all were touched by the Master. Like the Pied Piper, He walked up the path into His kingdom surrounded by His children.

"You receive what you believe," He declared. The more I believed that Jesus was showing me His glorious kingdom, the more I was able to receive the fullness of the revelation. The greater my faith was the deeper, more detailed, and far greater was the intensity of what I saw with my spiritual eyes.

"Receive what you believe," the Lord told the two blind men who came to Him. Both saw clearly. Both believed fully in Jesus' power to heal and open their eyes. (See Matthew 9:27-30.) Let us believe that He will freely open our spiritual eyes to see the wonders He wants to show us. Also let us believe that our ears will hear Him speak more clearly, and our mouths will speak His words with far greater accuracy. Let us have faith that He will not only show us great and awesome things, but that He will use us to do great and awesome things as well. Oh, Lord, increase our faith that not only will we see, hear and speak far deeper revelations, but that we will have a far deeper level of faith to heal the sick and receive miracles on behalf of your children.

Today I learned that we really do receive what we believe. Our unbelief limits what God can do for us, through us and with us. Nothing is impossible for those who believe.

The Unwanted Ones

Continuing to peer into the spirit realm, with eyes of faith opened wide, I saw a sea of little ones. They covered the rolling hills and dotted the landscape. The Lord gently touched my eyes, and the details in this vision increased. There weren't just thousands of children in heaven; I saw millions of children, even infants carried lovingly by beautiful angels. The Lord explained that most of these were those who were rejected and killed before their birth by their parents. Abortion rights and laws had stolen the lives from millions of children.

My Lord explained: "Though the earth would not make room for them, nor protect their lives, I do. The moment the lives of these innocent ones are taken, I dispatch My angels to gather them to Me, for My kingdom was prepared for such as these. Yes, it is these tender little ones that I take great delight in. They will grow and mature in My kingdom. Some will rule in the age to come over kings and kingdoms. Not one has escaped My care. All are here, no matter what the condition of their parents. Heaven was made for the pure and the sinless. Readily each one has embraced My Son, as their Lord and Savior, upon meeting Him as they entered My kingdom. They knew they were created by Him and for Him. What the enemy has meant for harm by killing them, I have turned around for their good.

"Every soul is precious to Me. I do not consider any worthless," He declared with such passion, it brought tears to my heart and my eyes.

As I pondered these words, I thought of this Scripture: *Jesus said, "Let the little children come to me, and do not hinder them, for the kingdom belongs to such as these" (Matthew 19:14).* Imagine! His kingdom belongs to children. It is theirs and was made for them. They are not thought of as an inconvenience or a noisy bother. On the contrary, they are held up as an example for all to follow.

His love and admiration for children is evident in this encounter Jesus had with His disciples. One day His followers were arguing about who was the greatest in His kingdom. Jesus brought a little child forward and had this child stand among them.

And he said: "I tell you the truth, unless you change and become like a little child, you will never enter the kingdom of heaven. Therefore, whoever humbles himself like this child is the greatest in the kingdom of heaven" (Matthew 18:3-4).

Not only are children accepted in heaven, but one of the prerequisites of coming into His kingdom is becoming like a little child. Though we don't have to return to our childhood and become children, we are expected to emulate the qualities of a child. Children are embraced in heaven; they are treated as something of great value.

I had always believed that once a child died and went to heaven, it instantly became an adult. From my visits to heaven, I know now that the Lord will not allow the enemy to rob His little ones of their childhood. What we experience growing up defines our character and often shapes us into who we become. The foundations of our lives, the formative years, are precious to the Lord. He will not let the enemy steal these years from His children nor allow him to take any part of their identity from them. Instead these children grow up in heaven surrounded by His love and guided by His presence.

Fully understanding my thoughts Jesus asked: "My daughter, are you surprised to see children in My kingdom? Don't children fill you with joy on the earth? Why wouldn't My kingdom be filled with babies and little ones for all to enjoy?"

He added: "These precious ones are the innocent ones that were taken from the earth before their time. What the enemy meant for harm in their lives, I have turned around for good. Those killed or taken prematurely by sickness and disease by the evil one have been embraced by Me and well cared for. Their joy has been made complete."

Though it was wonderful seeing so many happy faces and fulfilled lives, it also disturbed me that there were so many who had been so easily discarded by those who should have loved and nurtured them. I also knew that those who danced and played before me were but a small number of the countless ones who had entered the gates of heaven and grown up here. Now they were adults living full lives in His kingdom. Generations of those He rescued from before their birth dwelt in this paradise fit for a king. He truly is an amazing Savior!

Bending down and looking right in my eyes, my Friend explained that the children who had been aborted prayed for their parents and many had been saved as a result of their prayers. None were angry or bitter towards their parents, but all had been given the understanding of the Lord towards them. Instead of hatred, they felt His mercy. They knew how the enemy tricked and deceived their parents and understood fully what led them to abort their lives. Love was all they felt, and because love, pure love, motivated their prayers for their parents, they were very effective.

Someday there will be a great reunion when all are in heaven. There will be no shame or judgment, but instead, joy unspeakable. Love conquers all!

CHAPTER TEN

Riding on the Wings of the Spirit

Your eyes will see the king in his beauty and view a land that stretches afar (Isaiah 33:17).

One sunny morning, as was my daily custom, I sat in my prayer room with my Bible on my lap, my Christian music playing, and my journal and pen in hand. This was my time to spend with the Lord. Suddenly out of nowhere, I became increasingly overwhelmed by a great outpouring of God's love. The more I returned His overtures of love, the more intense His loving presence became.

I felt like Daniel when he encountered the majestic angelic being sent to him by God: *"How can I, your servant, talk with you, my Lord? My strength is going and I can hardly breathe" (Daniel 10:17).* His love so overwhelmed me, like Daniel, I could barely breathe.

Sitting quietly before Him, my spiritual eyes were opened, and I saw my Lord standing before me. With a gentle smile on His face and His arm extended to me, He invited me to come away with Him on a journey. With no hesitation, I immediately left the natural realm and walked away with Him into the spirit realm.

While we were joyfully walking along, He invited me to go for a ride with Him. As soon as the invitation was extended, two majestic, white eagles stood beside us: *...how I carried you on eagles' wings and brought you to myself (Exodus 19:4).* Turning toward them, we each climbed on the back of these magnificent, large birds. Once we were securely seated on their soft, yet sturdy backs, they took to flight and carried us high into the heavens. While flying beside Jesus, I saw the gleam of excitement in His eyes and heard His deep laugh. Immediately I knew this was going to be a wonderful revelation.

Leaving the earth, we ascended high over the expanse with nothing visible below us. Tightly holding onto the neck of this splendid eagle, I peered over his head and beheld a kingdom, exquisite beyond description, suspended in the air ahead of us. It looked like an enormous castle, more glorious than I could ever describe. I wondered how this other world I was approaching could be floating in the midst as it was.

Knowing My thoughts Jesus replied, "Does not your world hang in the air with nothing to support it? Why do you think it so strange that My world exists and was created to float in the air? Remember your world is but a faint reflection of Mine."

Awestruck as I listened to my Lord and looked down on the unique means of transportation I was flying to His kingdom on; I wondered, "Why an eagle, a beautiful, white eagle at that?"

Again demonstrating that my thoughts never escape His detection Jesus responded warmly: "No one comes into My kingdom unless they ride on the wings of My Spirit. I am the way, the truth and the life. No one comes to the Father but through Me. My Spirit leads everyone to Me and into My kingdom. Again I say, My Spirit guides all mankind to Me."

Listening to His patient explanation, I remembered the story Jesus told of Lazarus and the rich man. In this story, the rich man was in hell suffering while Lazarus was at Abraham's side living a joy filled life. Between the two there was a great expanse that separated them. Today I realized that I was flying in the spirit, through that expanse of darkness, on the wings of His Spirit. (See Luke 16:19-28.)

The Glorious Entrance to His Home

The closer we drew near to the enormous, golden castle suspended high in the atmosphere, the greater the feeling of warmth and all-consuming love became. This powerful love intensified continuously until we landed. After descending off the white eagle's back, I could barely stand on my feet because the feeling of this overwhelming love was so impacting. Looming before me at the entrance to His home were incredibly majestic walls, which appeared like they were made of mother of pearl. A beautiful rainbow-like color glimmered through them.

Filled with awe, I approached the immense doorway that welcomed all who beheld these iridescent walls surrounding the kingdom within them. Directly in front of the entrance were two glimmering gold steps. Unable to resist the impulse to feel what these magnificent stairs felt like against my cheek, I knelt down, bent over and put my face upon them. Soft, completely inviting, and filled with a love that made my heart dance, is the only way I can describe these golden steps. *...and saw the God of Israel. Under his feet was something like pavement made of sapphire, clear as the sky itself (Exodus 24:10).*

Gently Jesus reached down and lifted me back to my feet, "Come I have much more to show you, so that you can tell others of the magnificence of the kingdom I have prepared for those who love Me."

Enthralled, I gazed up at the doorway and noticed that the top of the entryway was made of one enormous emerald and the sides of two, long, shimmering rubies. Apparently the few gems that we have on the earth are but tiny fragments of the extravagantly large and exquisite ones here in Jesus' home. To my amazement, the doorway was wide opened with no door or gate to keep anyone out. Not only was there no door, but contrary to what I had expected, there were no angels with large threatening swords stopping anyone from entering. Everyone who was brought here by the Spirit of Jesus had immediate access into His kingdom.

Greeted by His Friends

With great awe, we stepped through the doorway. As we did, immediately a large host of angels signaled the Lord's entrance by blowing their long, gold, melodious horns. Jesus was so happy and relaxed. He was home.

Not only did angels greet His arrival with their harmonious musical announcement, but little children ran gleefully to Him.

They embraced Him like a child does when their father arrives home from a long day at work. Each one had something important to tell Him. One showed Him the colorful butterfly he was playing with. Another took Him by the hand and dragged Him over to a tree that the child had learned to climb that day. Jesus, full of joyful enthusiasm, climbed up to the top of the tree with the little boy and with many of the other children who accompanied this little one.

What a sight I stood back and watched: Jesus and many young children climbing a tree together, picking delicious fruit, and eating it as they laughed and talked to one another. Jesus was totally absorbed in these little ones' affairs. Each child was given His undivided attention. If they told Him about a rabbit they played with or a giraffe they rode on, He listened intently and acknowledged what they said by asking them to show Him. Off they went together into the gardens where the children played.

Animals were the children's playmates in this world of wonder. A glistening pond surrounded by colorful gardens and doting angels invited the youngsters to come for a swim. As many of the giggling children responded and ran into the pond, those kind and caring angels stood attentively by, waiting to wrap each one in a soft, fluffy towel. There was no disorder or confusion here. What I observed, with utter amazement, was a peaceful scene filled with love and laughter: no tears, no sorrow, no pain and no one feeling left out or unimportant.

After Jesus played with His children, He returned to me. I couldn't speak. The emotional scene I had just been honored to see had overwhelmed me.

Jesus' love and provision for these humans was beyond what I ever imagined. How could a God as great as He love these creatures like He did? I always knew He loved us, but never had I ever grasped the depths of His devotion and untiring admiration.

And a highway will be there; it will be called the Way of Holiness. The unclean will not journey on it; it will be for those who walk in that Way; wicked fools will not go about on it. No lion will be there, nor will any ferocious beast get up on it; they will not be found there. But only the redeemed will walk there, and the ransomed of the Lord will return. They will enter Zion with singing; everlasting joy will crown their heads. Gladness and joy will overtake them, and sorrow and sighing will flee away (Isaiah 35:8-10).

The Crying Woman's Story

Leaving the little children, Jesus took me by the hand and brought me to see a beautiful young woman. She had long, wavy, blond hair and wore a floor length, white dress. Though her apparel was not opulently embossed with gems, it was still elegant. Studying her face carefully, I tried to see if I ever knew her, but she did not look at all familiar.

She began to speak: "When I lived on the earth many years ago, I was filled with anger. If I had not repented before I died, I would not have made it into His kingdom. My heart was filled with poison against all who did not agree with me. I ruled harshly and bitterly. That is why my dress is plain. I did not let His love pour out of me, nor was I a reflection of His goodness. If it were not for His love and mercy, I would not have changed my heart before I died, and this would not be my final resting place."

Looking intently at this beautiful woman, I saw tears flowing down her cheeks. I recalled that Scripture says that in heaven there would be no tears, so I wondered why she was crying.

Knowing my thoughts she responded: "These are not tears of sorrow that I am shedding, but rather they are tears of devotion. I do regret the years that I spent on the earth hating instead of loving, denying the truths of my faith instead of following them. These tears are an expression of gratitude for the mercy I was shown. Just a simple turning of my heart from hatred to love, brought me out of eternal damnation to this glorious place of eternal life and joy. I did not deserve His forgiveness but truly earned His wrath.

"No one can understand the depths of His mercy and forgiveness unless they experience it firsthand," this beautiful lady explained. "I weep with joy for the unmerited love He extended to me. I did nothing to earn the glories of this place. Hatred filled my thoughts from morning till night. Schemes were manufactured to heap

115

vengeance upon those I hated. No good thing came forth from my life, but nevertheless I am here. I know my actions deserved a worse fate."

She continued: "Fear filled my heart as the days of my life drew to a close. The lessons I had been taught as a young child about the truths of Christianity haunted me. In His great mercy, He would not leave me alone. I dreamt of hell and knew it would be my final resting place. No good thing could I remember doing as I pondered my life's work. I was haunted by the evil deeds I had so callously done. But in the midst of these times of despair, I felt a tugging at my heart to turn to Him in sorrow for what I had done. I remembered Mary Magdalene who had been a great sinner, too. Once she turned to Jesus, she was forgiven and restored. I began to want to be forgiven and cleansed of the filth that I felt was clinging to my heart.

"One night," she said quite vividly, "after a terrible dream, where I saw myself suffering in hell for all the spiteful acts I had performed, I cried out to Jesus for mercy. After I took that first step, the rest was quite easy. I cried and cried in sorrow for all the evil things I had done, thought, and said. As I cried, I knew I was being forgiven like a little child confessing his faults to his father. It was so easy once I took the first step of hating what I had done and reaching out to Him for forgiveness."

Answering my questioning thought she explained further: "I weep now, not in sorrow for all the good I could have done with my life instead of the evil I did, but I weep for joy that I was so easily forgiven and restored. I love my life here in His kingdom and treasure every second in His presence. My joy is complete in Him. No one deserves the bountiful blessings He has prepared for them, but least of all me. When I partake of His benefits, tears of gratitude escape from my eyes because of His great goodness. I am a friend of the King."

Jesus smiled at this beautiful lady, His daughter, with a twinkle in His eye that told her how precious and special she was to Him. Without speaking a word, He thanked her with a nod of His head, and we walked away. Her joy had been made full.

Now Jesus spoke; "I had to show you how deep My love is for all, not just those who strive to serve Me, but all are the recipients of My great undying devotion. The tears you saw her shed are but a reflection of the tears of joy that I shed at her redemption. My daughter returned to Me! That day is marked down forever in the journals of heaven.

"It is true," He said, "that her reward is not the same as those who serve in My courts and allow Me to love and live through them, because I am just. Justice demands a reward for the faithful who lay their own desires down to embrace Mine. Though her reward is meager compared to others, her joy has been made complete in Me."

...I am he who searches hearts and minds, and I will repay each of you according to your deeds (Revelations 2:23).

CHAPTER ELEVEN

The Outskirts of the Kingdom of Love

They will walk with me, dressed in white, for they are worthy (Revelations 3:4).

One day while in the spirit realm, to my great surprise, I saw myself clothed in an elegant, diamond covered, white gown and was sitting on a large rock in His kingdom. Captivated by the glamorous diamonds sparkling all over my dress, I looked up and realized that Jesus was sitting next to me enjoying my childlike pleasure in the awesome dress He had given me.

Knowing that I was about to ask Him the meaning behind this stunning garment He explained: "Each time you were transparent and allowed My love to flow through you to others, one of these diamonds was placed in your attire. I am faithful to reward My friends who diligently serve Me. Heaven is filled with My signatures of appreciation to those who steadfastly and diligently work for Me. I am allowing you to see a few of these gifts I have stored up in My kingdom for My children, so that you can bring an understanding to others of the magnificence of heaven."

My Friend asked: "If I would cover the streets in gold, why wouldn't I cover My saints in diamonds, rubies and emeralds? Why wouldn't I lavish them with homes filled with everything that pleases them? Why wouldn't I, when everything is at My disposal? I am not limited in My ability to give. I have created abundant wealth to bestow upon those who earned it by their obedience to Me. I will withhold no good things from My beloved. I am a generous bridegroom. My bride will be treated like a queen in My kingdom. Nothing you could ever imagine will prepare you for the opulence and the splendor of My kingdom. I am ready for My bride: to adorn her with My brilliance and bestow upon her the wealth of the nations."

Visiting His Garden

While listening to the Lord, as He explained the grandeur He has awaiting us, and admiring the dazzling brilliance of this dress I was wearing, a delightful aroma surrounded me. From the corner of my eye I could see flowers.

Getting up from the rock, Jesus and I began walking along together. Beside the road we were walking on were the loveliest scented flowers I had ever seen: Red roses so perfect, they looked like they were made of silk velvet. Their leaves glistened like green satin. Daisies of every color, morning glories, daffodils, gladiolas, on and on, for as far as I could see; flowers filled the landscape. Colors blended together in an array of beauty, even more striking than a brilliant rainbow.

A gentle breeze that flowed from Jesus caused the flowers to sway, while a sweet melody came forth from them and intermingled with their fragrance. Love for Jesus seemed to be pouring out of these joyful flowers. They were alive with His love. As I looked at this magnificent colorful scene, I could feel the embrace of Jesus coming through the flowers.

The melody that came forth from them was enhanced by the songs of charming birds and the beauty of the butterflies that flew over and amongst this delightful, expansive garden. What a wonderful exchange of love I was observing. The flowers and the birds loved Jesus, and each other, as Jesus poured His love out on them. Jesus noticed everything wonderful about each flower, every bird and every single butterfly. Radiating His love and approval, smiling, He reached out His hand and gently touched the tops of the flowers. Incredibly, all I could feel was love.

Putting His arm around my shoulder Jesus said, "My kingdom is made of love. Everything here reflects My beauty and My love. Just the opposite is true of Satan's kingdom; hate emanates from everything there."

I remembered the awful scenes I had observed in hell on a visit in the spirit. Just a few weeks before this glorious divine encounter, the Lord appeared to me and took me into the deepest darkness of hell. So much blackness and despair, horrible sounds, putrid odors--nothing like the beauty of the sight I had just seen and felt today.

As I walked with Jesus, trying to erase the memory of hell from my thoughts, I realized that through this myriad of cascading flowers and soft, sweet music, unimaginably, I felt like heaven thought I was special because I was a friend of His.

The Father Speaks

Unexpectedly the Father spoke softly to my heart: "Everyone who loves My Son is treated like a queen in My kingdom. Because you have never seen Him as He is, but have believed in Him and given up all to be His, you are honored in heaven. Everyone who loves My Son on earth is loved here by all.

"Love is the music of My kingdom," He explained. "Love is the fragrance that pours out of the flowers in heaven, and love is the color of the flowers here as well. You were touched by My love, as you observed this beautiful garden on the outskirts of My kingdom. All who enter into My kingdom are greeted by My love expressed in the beauty of all that I created here to bring you enjoyment. It is all about My love for My creation."

An immense desire filled my heart. All I wanted to do was lie down in this vibrant garden and absorb all of this effervescent love pouring out of the flowers. Knowing exactly what I was thinking, the Lord encouraged me do just that. He knew I was afraid that I would crush the delicate flowers under me as I rested on them, but He told me that they would be fine. Immediately I stopped walking and lay down amongst these magnificent flowers. It felt like I was reclining on a soft bed of love; never had I felt so cherished in my life.

While basking in the garden, a bird flew over me, and as he flapped his wings, the feeling of love increased dramatically. I felt a surge of love for those who had mistreated me during my life. Some of these gentle birds landed on me, and the love continued to intensify. An overwhelming desire to be a vessel of His love burst within me. All this love that I was being filled with must be poured out on others. I could not contain it but felt an urgency to give it to all I met. This was the work of His kingdom: receiving His love and letting it pour out to others. Receiving it was so easy.

Then Jesus instructed me: "Just as simple as lying on a bed of flowers filled with My love and having them permeate you with that sovereign love, just as easy is it to let that same love pour out of you to others. The secret is to visit My love garden often. Be filled to overflowing, and like a brook that is overflowing its banks, My love will pour out of you effortlessly. Did the flowers exert any effort to make you feel special or loved? No, it just exuded out of them to you. Be filled with My love daily, and you will be like a fresh, babbling brook bringing refreshing love to all who encounter you or like a fragrant flower spreading the perfume of My love."

The Velvety Gold Cushion

To my great delight, the visits to heaven continued. In a truly magnificent vision, I saw myself in heaven lying on a soft, gold cushion. Love permeated both the air about me and the soft, feather-like, gold material my face rested on.

Suddenly Jesus was standing next to me explaining that everything and everyone in heaven is filled with His love, because love created them.

He declared lovingly: "Animate and inanimate objects, as well, are all filled with My love here. Everything you touch oozes My love out of it. That is why there is so much unity and peace in My kingdom, because love created it. Love sustains it. Love keeps it alive and allows for its existence. Love dances upon every sound in heaven. My kingdom is a kingdom of love.

"No one ever becomes insensitive to the continual outpouring of My love through My creation here," my Lord said. "It is always new and always overwhelming. That is why there is no sorrow or suffering here; love flows constantly to a degree that is without comparison to anything experienced on the earth."

Jesus explained: "No love of a parent, spouse, child or friend compares to the intensity of My love that is eternally displayed continually in heaven. The love that is sought after on the earth can only be found here: unconditional, constant, enthusiastic love. Divine love sustains life here and produces joy unspeakable in every heart. All are made complete in this love, which accepts and never rejects. If My people realized the degree of love that all who enter My kingdom inherit when they leave the earth, there would be no sorrow when a loved one dies.

"When you visit here," He added, "I allow you to feel but a small portion of the love that fills My kingdom or you would find life unbearable on the earth. Everyone who comes to Me, through My Son, on the wings of My Spirit, will know this love."

Every breath I took filled my lungs with an overpowering love. The atmosphere of heaven is made of love. During this encounter in the spirit realm, with every breath I took, I was experiencing heaven on earth.

Still curious, I asked the Lord what this gold, cloud-like cushion was that I was resting on. Profoundly, He answered, "Love, My daughter, the very essence of heaven."

This loved filled cushion was a physical manifestation of the heart of God. As His love poured out of His heart for me, it became soft gold. I was resting on the bosom of God. Heaven is the heart of God.

My Teacher continued: "My love is so powerful, it creates. It is not a weak love but mighty, never to be destroyed or defeated. It is the power that raised My Son back to life. My love creates life and destroys death."

...the earth is full of his unfailing love. By the word of the Lord were the heavens made, their starry host by his mouth. But the eyes of the Lord are on those who fear him, on those whose hope is in his unfailing love, to deliver them from death and keep them alive in famine (Psalm 33:5-6, 18-19).

The Solemn Hush of Heaven

*Then I looked and heard the voice of many angels, num-
bering thousands upon thousands, and ten thousand times
ten thousand. They encircled the throne... (Revelation 5:11).*

Just a few days later, I found myself pondering His great love
for mankind. After a time of sweet fellowship, suddenly the room
seemed to light up with the light of His love. My Lord appeared. He
just walked into the natural realm and invited me to follow Him into
the spirit realm.

Not knowing where we were going, I immediately followed,
absolutely sure that He would show me something I would never
forget. Totally immersed in His love, we walked quietly together for
a short distance, and then to my great pleasure we just lifted off the
ground and flew into the heavens.

Breathtakingly astounded, flying with my hand in His, we entered
His homeland. Upon landing we walked into an enormous, elegant
room that was lined on each side with countless angels. Each and
every angel had a long, golden horn. The moment Jesus appeared,
in unity, they all blew their instruments loudly announcing His
arrival. Together, as Jesus and I walked down the angel lined hall,
they instantly stopped blowing their elegant, melodious horns. They
were completely still and silent, because they wanted to hear any
word that Jesus might speak. I was experiencing the solemn hush
of heaven.

Jesus was so important to the angels that they didn't want to
miss a word that He spoke. Nothing was more significant to them
than listening to their King. Awestruck by what I was privileged to
witness, I recognized the little importance we place on hearing Jesus
speak on the earth as compared to the attention that is given to Him
in heaven.

Questioning myself I wondered: "What would our lives be like
if we positioned ourselves to greet Him and silenced ourselves to
listen to Him speak?" I'm sure this would bring heaven to the earth.

The Wonders of Heaven Explained

Finally my Friend spoke: "Yes, My daughter, great is the honor that is given to Me in My kingdom. My angels serve in My courts with tremendous devotion. Their love for Me is not manufactured. They stand ever awaiting My arrival, so they can herald Me and pour their praises out over My head. Heaven is all about giving. As they give out to Me, I give My word and My love out to them. Everyone in heaven delights in giving. The pleasure of giving fills all in My kingdom. You saw reciprocal love being displayed as you walked into My kingdom. Love is so profound here; nothing on the earth can duplicate it. Love gives and expects nothing in return. That is the love that flows like a river throughout My kingdom."

And now I will show you the most excellent way. If I speak in the tongues of men and of angels, but have not love, I am a resounding gong or a clanging cymbal. If I have the gift of prophecy and can fathom all mysteries and all knowledge, and I have the faith that can move mountains, but have not love, I am nothing. If I give all I possess to the poor and surrender my body to the flames, but have not love, I gain nothing.

Love is patient, love is kind. It does not envy, it does not boast, it is not proud. It is not rude, it is not self-seeking, it is not easily angered, it keeps no records of wrongs. Love does not delight in evil but rejoices with the truth. It always protects, always trusts, always hopes, always perseveres. Love never fails (1 Corinthians 13:1-8).

CHAPTER TWELVE

Heaven's Waterfall Revisited

Then the angel showed me the river of the water of life, as clear as crystal, flowing from the throne of God and of the Lamb down the middle of the great street of the city. On each side of the river stood the tree of life, bearing twelve crops of fruit, yielding its fruit every month (Revelation 22:1–2).

Months after my visit to the outskirts of heaven, I realized that the memory of the elegant golden bridge and the sparkling waterfall surrounded with magnificent flowers and lush fruit trees was fading. I thought I would never forget what I saw, but as I tried to recall the details of this vision, I found that they were not clear.

Knowing my disappointment, my Friend brought me instantly into the spirit back to the golden bridge. To my amazement, it appeared even more magnificent than I remembered from my previous visit here. Standing on the inviting bridge, I looked down at the crystal-clear water. It was teeming with life. Colorful fish swam in the river, darting among the golden nuggets that were scattered on its banks. Laughing with delight, I looked for the mountain made of shimmering gold from which the waterfall fell.

As I look through eyes of faith, I not only saw the waterfall that made all others on the earth diminish, but I saw beyond it. Those things in the distance that I had seen on my previous visit here now appeared as clear as if it they were very close. The distance was magnified in my sight.

Beyond the golden mountains and majestic waterfall was a splendid castle. This castle was not made with bricks and mortar, but was fashioned in pure gold. It was enormous. Numerous large spires shot from its structure into the sky. The sky above held an enormous brilliant rainbow. The entire sky surrounding God's mansion was painted with this glorious rainbow. An ornate wall lined its perimeter. Stained-glass windows, etched in gold, fashioned out of shimmering gems, dotted the walls. A river of living water flowed forth from the front of the castle down the mountain to the valley beneath where I stood on the golden bridge. This was the house of God, from which the river of God flowed.

I was being given a glimpse of the truth that everything in heaven glorifies God and reveals who He is. The stately gold castle was a picture of God the Father ruling from His throne. The river flowing from His throne was a picture of the wonderful Holy Spirit; a River of life sent to refresh, strengthen, and purify all who receive Him. Then the golden bridge that allowed me access to this heavenly land was a picture of Jesus, my Savior. He is the bridge that unites heaven and earth. Where there was no way to heaven, He made the way.

God reveals himself through His Son, His Spirit, His Word, His creation, the entire world and through the invisible world of the spirit. He makes Himself known, so we have no excuse for not believing in Him as He is (see Romans 1:19–20).

I stood staring down at the river below. I just wanted to partake of what I knew the river held: more of His Spirit, the anointing of His power, His great glory, His tangible presence. Instead of leading me into the river, the Lord led me toward the mountain pass. Reluctantly leaving the bridge, Jesus and I walked on one of the many gem embossed paths to His Father's house sitting at the top of the mountain.

Lush, well-manicured gardens spread out for as far as I could see all the way up the mountain path. Fountains fed by the gleaming river were at the center of many of the scenic gardens. I knew that my desire for more of His Spirit, more of the anointing, could be satisfied if I just ran over to a fountain and allowed myself to be refreshed.

Looking at my Lord for permission to run to the closest fountain, I saw the gentle, loving nod of approval on His face. That was all I needed. Letting go of His hand, I ran to be filled by His Spirit. The closer I got to the fountain, the larger it grew. Not hesitating for even an instant, I stepped into the exquisite, gem laden fountain. Heavenly water rained down on me, while I danced in the knee-deep water. Freedom! Totally abandoned to my God and free from all cares, all inhibitions left me instantly. Instead a tender, warm love filled my emotions.

The Sanctifying Work of the Holy Spirit

The Lord revealed that these fountains were not accidentally placed here. No, they were strategically set in place to prepare all who were coming into the presence of the Father. All that distracted them from being totally absorbed in His presence was washed away. I was being prepared by the cleansing waters of the Holy Spirit for my divine encounter. My mind, heart and body were being set free. His thoughts were being exchanged for my thoughts, His ways for mine, His love for my indifference, and I loved it!

A familiar warmth engulfed me, as I reveled in the fountain's outpouring. Looking up, I saw my Friend standing right next to me under the refreshing shower of the gentle fountain. Such a smile of approval emerge from His face, it flooded my heart with joy.

He proclaimed: "Your desire for more of My Spirit delights Me and My Father and pleases My Spirit. The more you seek Me, the more you will find us. You can't seek for too much, nor can you come too frequently into My Father's courts. You are always welcome. Come boldly into My presence and receive all I have for you."

Together we left the fountain and walked toward the gold mansion. Ascending the mountain, I noticed that others were coming to visit their heavenly Father and were bathing in the surrounding garden fountains. I knew it was a necessary step to entering His courts. All the distractions from life were being washed away, so that spiritual eyes and ears could hear and see and receive.

The more I observed, the more I realized that these splendid heavenly fountains were of great significance. They represented the sanctifying work of the Holy Spirit. To sanctify means to consecrate or set apart for a sacred purpose. As we encounter the Holy Spirit, He sanctifies us. *God chose you to be saved through the sanctifying work of the Holy Spirit (2 Thessalonians 2:13).* The fountains are a picture of the Holy Spirit washing us clean to present us to the Father–holy and undefiled. Paul taught that the Holy Spirit is essential, *so that the Gentiles might become an offering acceptable to God, sanctified by the Holy Spirit (Romans 15:16).*

As we submerge ourselves in the presence of the Holy Spirit, He sets us apart for God. His Spirit prepares us to come into the Father's courts where we belong. Old evil mindsets are changed, as we sit with the Holy Spirit, and His thoughts become ours (see Isaiah 55). The impossible suddenly becomes possible. Fear transforms into faith. Poverty is swept away and prosperity gains entry. Hard hearts are softened and made pliable in the hand of God. Stubbornness is evicted and a meek gentle spirit is imparted. All this happens as we bathe in the awesome presence of the Holy Spirit. *And we, who with unveiled faces all reflect the Lord's glory, are being transformed into his likeness with ever-increasing glory, which comes from the Lord, who is the Spirit (2 Corinthians 3:18).*

No longer controlled by fleshly passions and living for the world, with all its carnal pleasures, those sanctified by His Spirit become spiritual men and women. Those who have set their affections on the Spirit are made righteous by the blood of the Lamb and sanctified by the Holy Spirit. All are prepared by God to come and sit with Him forever. Yes, forever, we can behold His image and receive His benefits here on the earth and in His glorious kingdom. We have access to the throne of God continually and are forever welcome, because He has given us the key to His home.

A Visit with my Father

As we approached the ornately carved front doors, with barely a touch of the Master's hand, these impressive doors opened. Angels lined the path and some began blowing long, golden horns announcing our arrival. Fear grips my emotions as we walked into our Father's castle. I felt unworthy and feared seeing God. Jesus, knowing my thoughts, explained that I would not be seeing God in His glory with my natural eyes, just His form with my spirit eyes. With His reassurance, fear diminished and curiosity took its place.

In the distance I saw a massive throne and heard my Father welcome me: "I have been awaiting your arrival with great eagerness. Come sit beside Me. I have much to talk with you about; I want to explain My ways."

Days before our meeting, I had been wondering why those who had committed heinous crimes were not found guilty. It seemed like a travesty of justice. Knowing that this concerned me He said: "When you see those who are apparently guilty of a terrible crime set free, know that I desire the repentance of sinners more than I desire their punishment. It is the love and the grace of God that brings men to repentance (see Romans 2:4). My ways are not the ways of this world. I have come to seek and save those lost in sin. Forgiveness is My way."

Though I felt like I was alone visiting with my Father, His house was filled with those who loved Him. A vast multitude of people and angels filled the expanse around us. No matter how many loved and worshiped Him, He treated each one like they were all important to Him.

He explained what I was experiencing; "That is the love of a devoted Father that you perceive. I am devoted to all My children. I care for each one like they were an only child. Every concern they have, I care about."

While we visited together, He gave me a glimpse of His power, the same power that raised Jesus from the dead and created the world. He declared: "Power lives in you and is accessed by faith in Me. I have placed My power in the inner being of My children who love and serve Me wholeheartedly. Sadly few are fully aware of it and do not use the power I have given them. If they did, their lives would be full of victory. Defeat would be far from them. Sickness and poverty would not rule over their lives.

"You must know by faith who you are in Me," He said. "You must let the knowledge of My power direct your thoughts, actions and words. It is those who know My power that have been able to operate in it."

After speaking to me for a while, My Father stood to His feet. When He stood I thought, "Wow, you walk and have a body like ours!"

Reading my mind our Father replied, "Of course! I made you in My image; you reflect My glory." (See Daniel 7:9–10.)

Then He led me past all the people gathered about Him, down a few stairs, into a large private room. I wondered what this room represented. It was beautiful, but not as elegant as the throne room, more homey like a den. It had large windows on three of its walls that overlooked the world. Different scenes from the earth were displayed through each one. He forever watches over us.

Then He invited me to sit beside Him on a very comfortable soft couch. He and I were alone. It felt as though we were in the inner court. I remembered the lyrics of the song: past the outer court, past the crowds of people, into the holy place. In this place separated from everyone and everything, His tangible presence increased measurably.

While sitting very close with my head resting on His heart, I brought all that concerned me to Him and He said, "Everything that troubles you concerns me. I will dispatch My angels to take care of each and every situation." His reassurance removed those issues that were distracting me; now my mind was free to receive His thoughts.

To my amazement, He told me that He was replacing my old ability to process revelation with a new sharper one: "You have been praying and believing Me for an increase in My gifts. Now receive a greater ability, a keener insight into the spirit realm. Revelation will come more quickly and more completely." Even as I sat in the spirit in the inner court, I began to see and understand spiritual truths in a deeper way.

"For those who will sit with Me," He said, "and pay the price of intimate fellowship, revelation will be given on earth, just like it is given in heaven."

The verse from the Lord's Prayer, 'thy will be done on earth as it is in heaven,' took on new meaning. In heaven without the Father speaking even a word, He communicates His thoughts to all in an instant. Incredible revelations are received with no effort.

His will is that all would know Him, and because we know Him, we would love Him and serve Him forever. As we enter the spirit realm in intimacy, we can receive fresh revelation to bring back to the earth to others.

A Field of Fresh Revelation

With the blink of an eye, I was no longer in my Father's castle but was walking with my Lord in a large field of wheat that was gently blowing in the wind. Each stalk held a head of wheat that, once processed, could nourish those it fed. Jesus took one of these heads of wheat in His hand and broke it apart so I could see the kernels of wheat hidden within.

My Lord then explained His ardent desire to share His ways and His thoughts with us: "This field represents the vast amount of revelations I have for those who would partake of it. Most are satisfied with the loaves of bread others prepare for them; how much they are missing! Imagine if each would come to Me daily and enter the field of fresh revelation. Over and above what they could imagine, I would share with them. There are not a chosen few that are invited to partake of fresh revelation of Me and My kingdom. No, all are called to come and eat, to come and be refreshed, strengthened and nourished.

"My Word is the standard by which all revelation must be judged, but it is not the full extent of what I want to show all who love and serve Me. I have so much more to say, and what I say will always agree with Scripture. It will never contradict it. Fresh manna, fresh revelation must not be spurned as unnecessary or unscriptural. If all that I have said, or have to say, was written down ... *the whole world would not have room for the books that would be written (John 21:25)*.

"Each revelation will unveil Me. This is the work of the Holy Spirit: to come alongside My people and reveal Me, the Son of God, and My Father to them. It gives the Spirit great pleasure to speak about Our wonders. And as He reveals Us to all who will listen, We unveil Him to each one.

"To disdain the work of the Holy Spirit is a grave injustice to the Trinity, for We are one. When you defend My Holy Spirit, you defend Me and My Father. When one rejects the Holy Spirit, then I and the Father are rejected as well, for We truly are one God. Defend Me, defend My Spirit and you defend My Father."

While walking through the grain fields, the Lord instructed me to lie down and listen. Without hesitating, I immediately rested upon the sheaves the Lord pointed to. As I lay there in the spirit, I could hear soft voices coming forth from the surrounding wheat.

I heard: "Listen with expectant faith, for My Spirit is going to reveal a hidden truth to you. All who come hungry to know Me will receive a deeper revelation of who I am. Have faith, My friend."

Then a wonderful truth was imparted to me: "The Trinity is the pattern for the human family. The heavenly Father represents the father or head of the household. He is the provider, the protector, the voice of authority. The Holy Spirit is the pattern for the mother. She is the life giver, the guide, the counselor, the comforter, just like the Holy Spirit."

Immediately I understood: The job of the Holy Spirit is to reveal Jesus to us, to teach us His ways, as is the role of the mother in the family. Jesus represents the children in the family. He dutifully obeys all that the Father tells him to do. He did only those things He saw His Father do. He is the firstborn of many brothers or heirs. Jesus, the older brother, has shown us the way back home to the Father's house.

He has forged the way for us to be happy and successful. He came so that our joy would be complete. When He left the earth, He sent the Holy Spirit to mother us. The Holy Spirit guides us continually, lives in us and showers His love on us like a doting mother cares for her beloved child.

Just lying on the small section of the wheat field benefited me greatly. Now I had a clearer picture of the wonderful Godhead. I understood who the Holy Spirit was with a far greater clarity than I had previously. All creation reflects His glory and reveals who He is—even the human family.

Soaked in His Glory

As I entered the spirit, His glory fell and cloaked me in His love. Lost in His presence, I saw a magnificent tree. This tree was in heaven. It grew very close to my Father's palace. Because it was so near Him, it was soaked in His glory. The tree looked something like a weeping willow tree, but it was covered with diamonds. It looked like a stately tree after an ice storm in New England. Every branch and leaf was enshrouded in diamonds. It appeared that the diamonds were melted all over the tree and left to harden.

"This is a picture of what happens to those who come near to Me on a regular basis," my Friend explained. "As you see, this tree is planted beside My home. It is immersed in My glory continually and now reflects My glory for all to see. Those who dwell in the secret place of the Most High will reflect My goodness, My love, My compassion and My great glory! No longer is this just a simple tree; now this tree is diamond laden. One who spends time in My courts will be glorified as well."

In my previous visits to heaven, I saw many magnificent trees but none resembled this one. Never did I see one that was cloaked in diamonds and that glistened in the light of His glory. The Lord explained that none of those trees I had seen were planted beside His home. They were glorious but weren't soaked in His continuous glory like this one was. I want to be like that diamond drenched tree planted beside My Father's house: continually soaking in His glory, constantly in His presence.

CHAPTER THIRTEEN

The Hall of Miracles

After this I looked, and there before me was a door standing open in heaven. And the voice I had heard speaking to me like a trumpet said, "Come up here, and I will show you what must take place after this" (Revelation 4:1).

In an astounding vision, as in past encounters, I saw myself dressed in the elaborate, white, diamond covered gown, but to my utter dismay, I was walking in the spirit upon a path that was full of snakes. Fearfully I kept my eyes glued upon these snakes while I walked on their backs. With immense relief, I noticed they were all dead. Looking up, I realized that Jesus was walking beside me. Despite the conditions of the path we were walking upon, I could feel the Lord's joy and expectancy at what He was about to reveal to me.

When we reached the end of the snake strewn path, we ascended gold steps and walked through a wide, ornate corridor that was lined with many rooms. Overcome with excitement, I started running down the wide hall, looking curiously into the rooms.

To my wonder, the first room was filled with body parts: eyes for the blind, ears for the deaf, tongues for the speechless, legs for the lame, strong healthy bones for the arthritic and others too numerous to list.

The next room I peered into had wheelchairs, crutches, walkers and other devices that were no longer needed. This room appeared to be a memorial to a fantastic victory over diseases and deadly afflictions.

Unable to contain my excitement, I ran with great elation to the next room. This one was filled with hearts, only hearts. I knew they were going to be given to people who would be turning their lives over to Jesus. He was going to give them hearts for Him.

Backing out of this doorway, I quickly advanced across the hallway into the next room. This room was filled with countless little children. They represented vast multitudes that were going to be birthed into God's kingdom soon.

The next room I peeked into was filled with pure white doves. Immediately I knew that the Holy Spirit was going to be sent to millions as we prayed for His release. What excitement filled my heart while I ran from room to room upon the shimmering golden floor! Joyfully I noticed that the gold walkway was so pure, it shone like a mirror.

Approaching the next doorway, I looked inside and saw a room filled with empty hospital beds. Jesus' joy at these empty beds was contagious. I began to laugh, knowing the joy He felt for His friends that were going to be healed.

Still advancing down the hall, laughing the entire way, I entered another room where the impossible was made possible. All hurdles were easily surmounted.

Miracles Are Coming to the Earth

"The days ahead will be marked by the miraculous!" Jesus exclaimed. "Joy will captivate My children, as they watch multitudes come into My kingdom. Eye has not seen, ear has not heard, nor has it entered the hearts of man what God has prepared for those who love Him. Nothing is impossible for Me." (See 1 Corinthians 2:9.)

While Jesus spoke to me, He invited me to dance with Him in this golden hall lined with rooms of tremendous promise. "Trust Me to fulfill on earth what you have seen in heaven," He declared while we danced together. I kept hearing, "It will happen," over and over as a refrain while we danced and laughed together.

Looking into my eyes He explained: "Those things which kept you from fulfilling My purposes for your life are destroyed. I have given you a peek into the future. You overcame by the blood of the Lamb and the word of your testimony." (See Revelations 12:11.)

Now I understood what the dead snakes in the vision represented. Walking on them, on my way to this Hall of Miracles, showed that all the faults and failings in my life that were keeping me from fulfilling my call to walk in His full authority were destroyed.

Abruptly my thoughts shifted to the dress I was wearing. Though my dress was laden with thousands of gems, it was not heavy or cumbersome. Jesus explained that all things were made possible with Him in His kingdom, even making the heavy things light. I could see the dress in greater detail and noticed that an elaborate, red, ruby necklace adorned my neck. Love shown, prayers prayed; nothing escaped His appreciation, and the rewards were opulent and stunning.

With the customary gleam in His eyes, my King held me close while we danced in the splendid golden hall surrounded by the rooms filled with impending miracles. Curiously I asked Jesus which of the rooms was His favorite. Answering me, He explained that I had only seen a few of the rooms that were awaiting their release to the earth.

Whispering in my ear He said, "The season for their release is soon coming; the time is at hand for My great glory to be revealed. Each room is but a manifestation of My undying love for My children. When the heavens open and the gifts and blessings are bestowed upon all, the nations will know they are loved."

The room with the empty hospital beds kept coming to my mind. For some unknown reason, its presence in the hall drew me to it. Knowing my attraction to this room was so intense; Jesus led me back to it. Again I looked into the hospital room. The beds were in disarray, sheets pulled back like someone had just exited them. Not only were they messy and not made, but there were so many that filled this enormous room, they were stacked on top of each other.

Silence was not a part of this room. But instead of the quiet that I expected to hear and remembered from my quick peek on my previous visit, I heard sounds. Listening intently, I could hear children laughing loud squeals of delight. I heard belly laughs from grown men and laughter that was mixed with tears of joy from thrilled women. Though these people were not visibly there in this room filled with cumbersome hospital beds, the expressions of their satisfaction and joy were. I knew part of the vehement jubilation I was listening to was from the nurses and doctors who attended these patients before they were released from their illnesses by the Great Physician. This was my favorite room, and I wondered if it was Jesus' as well.

Visiting Jesus' Favorite Room

Immediately He responded, "Come, My curious friend, I will show you the room in this hall that pleases Me the most." Together we walked far down the hall, where I had not previously visited. Excitement welled up within my heart, because I knew that I was going to receive a deeper revelation of who my Lord was when I saw which room He valued the most. With eager anticipation, I noticed more sounds were coming from all the doorways as we quickly passed by them.

Finally we entered the room most cherished by Jesus. This was a room where the lonely and forgotten ones had once resided. It resembled a nursing home, but not all who were released from this room resided in nursing homes. In this place, joy was brought to the hearts of the forgotten, lonely ones who had been cast aside during their lives. Broken hearts were mended in this room: restored, refreshed and filled with a love that brimmed to overflowing proportions. Tears were wiped away and found here no more; tears that were shed, not just from weeping eyes, but tears that poured out of wounded hearts. This was the room beloved by Jesus.

As I watched Him walk about this room, His love for the broken hearted and for the neglected, forgotten ones was transparent before me. Empty rocking chairs scattered the room. Cardboard boxes, dirty mats and rags the homeless resided in and on were strewn about, just like they were left when their occupants were lifted out of them. Empty disheveled twin beds that came from tiny rooms were scattered about amongst the heap of chairs and empty boxes. This room looked like a dump. I could even see flies that used to dwell with these people searching for their companions.

Then I heard the sounds that the future would produce: exhilarated, joyful laughter, mixed with sobs of appreciation. Because the pain and the bondage were so great, the corresponding gratitude was expressed with such a depth of sincerity and heartfelt appreciation, it brought tears to my eyes. Now I understood why this room held such affection for Jesus. This was why He was sent to the earth, to rescue the downtrodden. It is still His heart's cry and top on His agenda of what He will accomplish during the great outpouring of His Spirit.

Again Jesus spoke, "Yes, My daughter, I am a friend to the lonely and those that have been cast aside. I never forget My children. Not one escapes My gaze, and I share their pain. Soon I will share their joy." With that remark, I saw a big smile back on my Friend's face.

Returning down the hall with Jesus, I realized that though the pain of a hurting, diseased racked body is awful, the pain of a broken hearted, lonely person is worse. All their pain does not escape His notice. His heart bleeds for them. *I know the Lord secures justice for the poor and upholds the cause of the needy (Psalm 140:12).*

My gracious King exclaimed, "Yes, My great desire is to relieve the intense suffering of the masses and to touch the hearts of individuals. I have come to wipe away every tear, and I will not rest until it is accomplished."

Smiling He took me in His arms, and we danced in joyful expectation of what will happen soon. *"In that day," declares the Lord, "I will gather the lame; I will assemble the exiles and those I have brought to grief. I will make the lame a remnant, those driven away a strong nation" (Micah 4:6-7).*

The Hall of Miracles Revisited

Weeks passed by and, once again, I found myself in the spirit in the Hall of Miracles. Standing on the translucent gold floor, I looked and saw the hall that seemed endless stretching out before me. As in the past, Jesus, my Lord, stood beside me. He invited me to look into a room that had escaped my scrutiny on my last visit here.

With eager anticipation, I ran over to the room whose door was opened and looked in. Hanging all about the room were fishing nets, golden fishing nets. These fishing nets were going to be released to the earth and sent to those found trustworthy, and appointed by Him, to gather in the great harvest.

Jesus declared emphatically: "The hour is at hand for the gathering of the great harvest. Just like I told Peter, I tell you, in the past you gathered in fish, or the things of the world, but in this hour you will gather in men. They will gladly come, rejoicing, into My kingdom. Running and skipping like little children, they will happily run into My waiting arms. Love will capture them and never let them go. I am releasing these nets to those appointed by My Father to gather My people to Me."

Then He added, "I have something else to show you." With that invitation, we walked together to the next room. My heart was beating loudly with excitement and anticipation. I could hear, ever so gently, the resound: "It is the hour; the time is at hand; the time has come--the time has come--the time has come..."

Amazed I saw a room empty, except for a great wind blowing within it. The wind blew, not cold and harsh, but warm and with great strength. Jesus explained: "The wind of My Spirit is about to be released as it was at Pentecost. The world is hungry for a move of My Spirit, and it is coming, for the time of waiting is over. The time is truly at hand for My Spirit to be poured out upon all mankind. What a wonderful hour you are living in, My friend. The hour when My great glory is going to be released upon the earth."

I wanted to step into the room and bask in the warmth of the wind of the Spirit. Jesus smiled and nodded, giving me the go ahead. He always knows what I am thinking. Sheepishly I entered the room, and His Spirit captured me in His warm embrace. Love like a mighty rushing wind flooded me. This love carried me about the room. So much love filled me; I wished I would never have to leave.

Jesus reminded me: "This very wind of My presence is about to be released to the earth. My angels are getting ready now, as we speak, to bring to the earth all the contents of these rooms. Miracles are going to break out everywhere, for the hour is at hand. My friend, you will experience the wind of My Spirit on the earth."

His comforting promise made it easier for me to leave this room that was brimming over with the winds of love. Now I knew what those gathered in the upper room felt when the mighty, rushing wind blew into that room. Love flooded them!

When the day of Pentecost came, they were all together in one place. Suddenly a sound like the blowing of a violent wind came from heaven and filled the whole house where they were sitting. They saw what seemed to be tongues of fire that separated and came to rest on each of them. All of them were filled with the Holy Spirit and began to speak in other tongues as the Spirit enabled them (Acts 2:1-2).

Days Later another Visit to My Favorite Place

"It is time for these doors to be flung open and for all the contents in these rooms to be sent to My children," I heard my Lord declare, as I found myself in the spirit realm standing once again in the Hall of Miracles. "As each prayer is prayed, as each declaration of faith is spoken, angels are dismissed to implement all and more. Yes, I say, and more, because over and above what each one asks for will be given to them. This hall does not just contain miracles for healing, but all My children need for a full and happy life lies here."

Instantly I saw the heart of Jesus. The Hall of Miracles resides within His heart. All that was deposited in each life was a tangible expression of His abundant love. All came forth out of His heart to heal, to transform and to bless. Families and friends were reunited, marriages healed and restored, finances blessed and increased, homes rebuilt. On and on–all that was needed to bring joy and completion to His loved ones was here.

In the past on my visits to this hall in heaven, I saw many rooms filled with different items. Then, more recently, I saw the same rooms; many were emptied of their contents. To my delight, today I saw the Hall of Miracles with far greater clarity. It was not like a hall in a large building as I had previously thought; today I saw its reality. It was miles long. My eyes couldn't see the end of it.

His arm is not too short to bless us. Far beyond what we could ever think or imagine are those blessings He has set apart for His loved ones. As I walked down this winding hall, I realized that there was no end to it. Impulsively I asked my Lord if I could look into some of these rooms. "Of course," He replied with an enormous gleam in His eyes and a gregarious smile on His lips.

The first room I ran to was filled with gifts piled from floor to ceiling. All were exquisitely wrapped. This room, like the hall, was enormous. The packages, all different, all elaborate, were so numerous that there was barely room for me to walk amongst them.

"These gifts represent surprises I sent, and will send to those who love and serve Me," He said. "Some are homes sold. Others are new cars that were thought impossible to get."

He explained that those presents represented our secret heart's desires which often go unexpressed, because they appear out of our reach. How are Lord delights in giving us these surprises! I could see it on His smiling face; a smile that originated in His heart.

Then I heard: "People are going to pray with faith in this hour, and those things that were held here will be, at long last, released to them. Faith will be made available to them; that faith that moves mountains and activates the miraculous."

With my mouth aghast, I walked throughout this room which resembled an enormous storehouse or warehouse. I saw houses stacked on top of each other awaiting their call to the earth. Cars, all kinds and colors, were neatly and carefully piled high. As I made my way through the maze of merchandise, I came upon rows of bicycles, motorcycles, racks of clothing and elegant shoes. Jewelry filled many cases and shimmered in the light of His presence. Furniture, rocking chairs, recliners and new bedroom sets appeared to stand at attention as we walked past them.

Just seeing what was awaiting God's people filled me with a new found faith. I knew what He wanted to give us, if we would just believe and ask. Then He could give us these wonderful, extravagant surprises.

As I remained standing in awe in the room of His surprises, I heard my Lord explain: "When you look and see all the gifts I have stored up for My children, know that you are seeing My grace. This room truly represents My loving favor, My unmerited, unearned blessings. These are held here for all who will believe in Me and in what I will do for them."

Breathless I wondered at the majesty and opulence of His great grace. Instead of receiving what we deserve, He delights in showering upon each of us His best.

He explained: "If I gave each one what he deserves, then how would I differ from mankind? It is an easy thing to exact an eye for an eye, or a tooth for tooth. To give extravagantly to those who despitefully use Me is who I am. I am gracious and compassionate, full of mercy towards all, not just those who merit it. I am the hand of He who lifts up those who beat Me and thrust Me to the ground. I am the God who blesses and forgives those who despitefully use My beloved friends. No offense is too heinous for Me to forgive fully.

"My forgiveness is supernatural," Jesus declared. "It does not just excuse wrongs, but it goes the next step. It blesses those who deeply offend Me and Mine. I am the hand that covers a multitude of sins and embraces wholeheartedly. I am the hand that restores those things lost or stolen by the enemy, when each wandered far from Me. Not only do I restore, but I open the windows of heaven and pour out My blessings, My great grace. Look around you and see the evidence of My grace. See those you determine are unworthy of blessings be prospered. I delight in extending grace to all (see John 3:16).

"Do the same," He continued. "Give My grace to those who have not earned it. Give acceptance, forgiveness, loyalty, friendship, concern and prayers. Bless with your best, as I do." *For the law was given through Moses; grace and truth came through Jesus Christ (John 1:17).*

Jesus concluded our visit with this sure promise: "Miracles will happen as you obey Me and extend grace with a heart of love (see Luke 15). Wholeheartedly forgive! Gregariously bless! Show mercy to those who deserve judgment. Lift up the forlorn with the word of love. Care for those who ignored you in your time of need, and watch as I open the windows of heaven over both of your lives. Watch; just stand back and watch as I heal and bless through you. As you extend unmerited love, you will receive an abundance of My unmerited love in return, for I do bless those who bless others."

CHAPTER FOURTEEN

The Sea Of Love

See, the Lord rides on a swift cloud... (Isaiah 18:4).

Looking into the spirit, I witnessed Jesus walking up a very steep incline. The sun was shining so brightly, it was difficult to see His form.

He joyfully called me to follow Him, "The time is short, My friend. Come quickly. Don't worry about stumbling on the rocks along the way, because I have cleared a path for you to follow Me easily." His joy was contagious, and I started laughing as I ran after Him in the gleaming sunlight.

"When I bring you before a door," He began to council me as we walked together, "and it appears to be opening, you must go through it without hesitation. It is like the rock strewn path you have encountered on your walks with Me. When I desire you to go a certain way, I clear the path and make it possible. Come, as I beckon you, through possibilities I present to you. Don't hesitate, because the time is short, and there is much to do in the days ahead. Yes, they will be days filled with My great glory, but they will require diligent service as well. Come, we are reaching our destination."

Just as He was speaking these words, I saw the crest of the hill. It appeared to be grassy and inviting. Again He beckoned me, "Come, I want to show you a part of My kingdom that will give My children great happiness."

A Foretaste of What is to Come

As we climbed the hill together, I remembered the day He brought me to the entrance of heaven, and I observed beautiful gardens where children played with the angels and the animals in heaven. This was not the same place. Nor was it the same place called the outskirts of heaven, where I enjoyed the lush fields of fragrant flowers and basked in their love, along with the love of the birds and the butterflies.

Continuing along, we walked in the sunlight through a field filled with wheat. This wheat field moved gently with the breeze and seemed to respond to Jesus when He placed His hand upon the tops of the stalks, while He walked through the field. As I walked behind Jesus through this magnificent sea of wheat, a wonderful fragrance of freshly baked bread filled my nostrils. The bright sunshine, the elegant stalks of wheat, the aromatic scent of bread and Jesus' sweet presence made me want to stop and lay down in the wheat field, just like I did in the field of flowers.

But Jesus coaxed me, "There is no time to stop now, My friend. Come, you have not seen all that I have to show you today. Come!" I was not tired from our journey through the wheat field, but just wanted to savor the moment here with Jesus. He knew what was in my heart, and it pleased Him. Encouraging me, He added, "Come, this is but a foretaste of what I have to show you."

After questioning Jesus as to why the wheat seemed to respond to His touch, He answered, "Everything in My kingdom responds to My touch. My life and My love fills everything here."

Leaving the wheat fields, we walked into a field filled with elegant flowers of every kind and color. Acres and acres of magnificent, fragrant flowers surrounded me. Not only did they smell and look beautiful, but they were exquisite to the touch as well. Putting my face close to them to take a deep breath of their aroma, I heard a sweet melody emanating from them. They were singing a love song to Jesus that I was being allowed to hear.

The Place of Solace and Comfort

Softly Jesus explained, "When the suffering I endure from seeing My children reject Me on the earth becomes unbearable, this is the place I come to for solace and comfort. In My kingdom everything and everyone loves Me."

Beyond the vast field of the exquisite loving flowers, I saw water gleaming and birds singing, while they flew above the crystal clear lake. Merrily approaching this glorious body of water, I was amazed to see numbers of fish jumping out of the sea. They were greeting Jesus. He walked right into the water and received the cheerful welcome of the sea creatures all about Him.

I thought of the vast number of fish Peter caught when Jesus told him to lower his nets in the Sea of Galilee. Incredibly these fish were beyond number and greeted Jesus like a dog greets its master. Playfully placing His hands upon them, they gleefully received His love. Turning, Jesus invited me to join Him in the Sea of Love. The warmth and the love that was present in the waters filled my being, as I walked and swam over to my Friend.

With the sparkle reflected off the crystal, blue water glistening from His eyes He told me: "Often I tell you to get apart with Me, so I can fill you with My love and heal your wounds. I practice what I preach. This is one of the places I come to in My kingdom where I receive the refreshing touch of My Father through His creation. His love fills everything here. When no man reaches out to Me in love and worship, I come here to be satisfied. The longing in My heart to be loved must be fulfilled."

Pondering the seriousness of His words, Jesus and I left the refreshing waters and sat on the sandy shore, absorbing the warm, drying rays of the sun. The love that filled me made every moment of sorrow I carried in my heart disappear, even the new sorrow I felt for my often neglected Friend. Jesus was showing me the secret to His abounding joy and peace.

"You, too, can feel this same love," He encouraged me, "anytime you come into My presence."

Now I knew why Jesus was in such a hurry to ascend the steep hill we climbed to get here. He was in a tremendous hurry to absorb

His Father's love which shone through the wheat, the flowers and the sea with its loving creatures in and above it.

"Love heals every wound," Jesus explained. "Love fills every cavity of loneliness and relieves the pain of unrequited love and rejection. Love brings joy in the morning after an evening of sorrow. Love wipes away every tear and causes the forlorn to smile. Love is the fuel and the fire of My kingdom. Love brought everything into being and sustains the life of My creation. Only love is needed, only love. In My kingdom there is only love. There is no wrath or violence, no jealousy or contention, only love."

While I lay on the beach with my Friend, a bird came over to me. Expecting the bird to peck me, I immediately became afraid. Instead the gentle little bird pressed its cheek against mine and softly rubbed its delicate feathers against my face. It was so unlike anything I ever experienced on the earth.

"In My kingdom," He said, "nothing has been spoiled by sin. Only love fills My creatures. Love alone pours out of them to one another. Come to Me often, so that I can touch you and fill you with My Father's love. Then you can give that love to those in need of His touch."

The tender bird lay down beside my face and softly rubbed my cheek. All the time it did this, I could feel love being poured into my heart. Jesus smiled a knowing smile at me and held my hand in His while love healed my heart.

Explaining further, He said: "On the earth there are many of My creatures and creations that are especially gifted with My love. Children, adults, pets, fragrant flowers, melodies and even fragrances can be used by Me to pour My love into those who are willing to receive it. The principles that exist in My kingdom are reflected on the earth. Though imperfectly, they are still alive and present on the earth. Be open to receive the outpouring of My love wherever and whenever it flows to you. Also, be ready to let My love flow from you to others."

You are the light of the world. A city on a hill cannot be hidden. Neither do people light a lamp and put it under a bowl. Instead they put it on its stand, and it gives light to everyone in the house. In the same way, let your light shine before men, that they may see your good deeds and praise your Father in heaven (Matthew 5:14-16).

CHAPTER FIFTEEN

The Place of Divine Consolation

For I am convinced that neither death nor life, neither angels nor demons, neither the present nor the future, nor any powers, neither height nor depth, nor anything else in all creation, will be able to separate us from the love of God that is in Christ Jesus our Lord (Romans 8:38-39).

"Come, what I have to show you today is more magnificent than anything I've shown you in the past," I heard as I sat before my Friend in prayer.

Carefully He led me into a forest of lush, deep green foliage. Leaves that sprung from the gigantic trees that were assembled there were larger than an umbrella. The fragrance of this incredible forest delighted me so much, I found myself taking deep breaths. I wanted to capture as much of this scent as I could. It smelled like life, vibrant life growing everywhere.

Lagging behind and totally lost in the moment, I hoped I'd never forget this scene or the delightful fragrance here. Startled by His gentle whisper, Jesus leaned over and encouraged me to follow Him. Filled with expectancy, I placed my hand in His and quickly ran beside Him. Instantly I felt the warmth of His love, as He smiled tenderly down at me. Walking briskly, we came to a cool, clear, running brook and easily climbed across it upon the rocks that made a natural bridge for us. After crossing the stream, we arrived in front of a steep wall that reached high into the sky. Jesus brought me to the side of the wall, which had a stone staircase built into it. Together we joyfully ascended the mountainous wall and Jesus asked, "Is this difficult or tiresome, My daughter?"

I blissfully responded that it was more fun than I had experienced in a long time. The thrill of discovery filled my heart, as I absorbed the majestic scenery surrounding us, while we scaled the steep, stone steps. During our ascent, when I was unable to see my surroundings clearly, the Lord instructed me to focus on Him. When I gazed upon Him, suddenly, I was able to see everything He wanted me to discover. I saw luscious, deep green ivy growing up the wall and brightly colored wild flowers springing through the cracks and spaces around us.

"Looking at Me is the secret of finding My treasures and discovering those things that are hidden from the world," my gentle Teacher explained.

Now I could see blue jays, cardinals, robins and eagles flying about us. I could hear their songs as I watched rabbits, snakes, lizards and grasshoppers enjoy their environment. The more I saw while looking through Jesus, the more my heart felt like it was being filled with overpowering love and joy. Jesus and I climbed and laughed, as we delighted in this wonderful scene. I was enjoying the climb so thoroughly that I completely forgot we were heading to a destination.

Laughing Jesus chided: "My child, many times you get so absorbed and intent upon where you are going, that you forget to enjoy yourself along the way. The path of your journey, to accomplish what I've given you to do, is meant to be part of the enjoyment that I want you to experience. If you are just goal oriented, you won't understand My ways, and you will miss a huge part of the experiences I've planned for you. Look to Me, and I will help you to relax and discover the joy of the journey."

I asked the Lord if this was His kingdom. He explained that it was the way to His kingdom, but that we hadn't arrived there yet. We continued to climb and enjoy one another's company, laughing the entire time.

Observing the Fullness of His Splendor

He continued, "The more you look at Me, the more you will see the beauty around you." I saw the gleam in Jesus' eyes, like diamonds sparkling in the light, and knew that what was ahead of us on this path was going to be delightful. "Remember to look at everything I show you through Me," He explained, "and it will enhance their beauty and deepen your understanding of what I am teaching you."

Looking up at Jesus, I saw the sky overhead. It was the color of transparent gold, so warm and inviting. My heart leapt within me at the expectation of what I would see over the crest of this mountain enshrouded in the golden sky above. Clouds seemed to dance at our feet. We had climbed so high, we were walking above the clouds into the realm of His glory. Joy overtook me, as I looked through Jesus' brilliant eyes at this extravagantly magnificent sight.

I focused my full attention on Jesus, and to my complete surprise and delight, we began to float in the air. Holding hands, we laughed together, as we easily ascended the stone mountain into the warm, golden sky above us. Love captured my heart and took my breath away. In this place high above the clouds, I became totally absorbed in Him. All I knew was His magnificent love; nothing else mattered. Tears of joy fell from my eyes, as the embrace of His love deepened.

Flying over the Mountains of Impossibilities

Higher and higher we ascended, and, at some point in time, while still holding hands, we began to fly. I felt like Wendy in the Peter Pan story, laughing in my new found freedom, flying in His love over the land below. "Now I want you to look down, My child," Jesus declared.

I looked and saw the tops of mountain ranges with soft clouds encircling them. I remembered the Scripture that says ... *if you have faith as small as a mustard seed, you can say to this mountain, "Move from here to there" and it will move. Nothing will be impossible for you (Matthew 17:20-21)*. I was flying over the mountain of impossibility beside Jesus, laughing merrily at the sight below. Each

155

mountain represented something I was concerned about or a trial I was going through in my life.

"Joy in the journey," I heard Jesus whisper in my ear. He was showing me the secret of having joy throughout the journey of life. I was flying high above my circumstances, laughing, filled with His love, focused on Him and not on my problems. Tears of joy fell from my eyes, as I laughed at the ease in which I was able to rise above everything into the glories of His presence. Nothing mattered but Jesus and being absorbed in His amazing love.

I saw large mountains become small hills while I happily flew over them with my Friend. The things that concerned me the most brought me the most joy when they diminished in size. I was surprised when I saw how many mountains filled the land below us. Jesus was showing me how many issues had filled my thoughts and troubled me. It was His great delight to diminish them and restore my joy to me.

When we reached the end of the mountain range, a deep peace flooded me. Below I saw rolling hills of different shades of green and brown. The brown patches of land were freshly tilled; fertile soil waiting for seed to be sown in them. These were areas that had been recently surrendered to Jesus by faith and trust and were ready for fresh manna, fresh promises from God, to be spoken into them.

Explaining what I was observing Jesus told me: "Every situation you surrender to Me is like these gardens I am showing you. Something that was hard and grueling to you, once I am allowed to govern it by your faith, hope and love will become a place of abundance. I turn problems into places of fertile hope and joy."

Now I looked down and saw a land covered with colorful, fragrant fruit trees of every kind. Angels dotted the landscape and picked the fruit that was ripe and ready for harvest.

"These fruit trees represent those issues that you've given to Me and left with Me to take care of for you," Jesus lovingly explained. "They are bearing fruit for your eternal reward. Today I have brought you to the place of Divine Consolation. With your eyes fixed on Me, I can take all that troubles you and turn these situations around to bring you peace and joy."

To my amazement, I observed my garden in heaven. It was already bearing fruit there, awaiting my arrival to receive my great reward. Just giving Jesus all, even my problems, produced magnificent blessings for me.

You did not choose me, but I chose you and appointed you to go and bear fruit--fruit that will last. Then the Father will give you whatever you ask in my name (John 15:16).

Another Heavenly Visit

"Keep your gaze heavenward," I heard as I saw myself step through a veil. In an instant, I left the natural realm and entered the spirit realm. I saw the brilliant, vibrant colors of heavenly flowers overshadowed by the light of heaven's glory.

"Don't just look; but smell the fragrance of heaven," my Friend declared. "Bask in the warmth of My love. Fully feel and enjoy! Allow your senses to partake of all that heaven holds. Then bring those delights back into your realm. Bring the joy, the satisfaction, the increased faith and the awe inspiring revelations back to share with others. All that I do on your behalf is for you to enjoy and then share."

My Savior's words prompted me to bury my face in a velvety blossom. Not only did I drink in the sweet fragrance, but I lavished myself with the soft texture of the elegant, creamy, yellow petals. Far more delightful than any perfume I had ever enjoyed, this flower's fragrance captivated me.

"Come," I heard, "I have much more to show you. Look!" Obeying my Lord, I removed my face from the flower's embrace and looked at the land before me. To my great delight, I realized that I was back on the flower laden hillside. The rainbow sky beckoned me to come and enjoy its beauty.

A bustle of activity filled the lush hillside. Families and friends laughed, played and picnicked together. Standing back quietly, I listened. Laughter and uplifting conversation filled the air. Love was being freely expressed with no restrictions or limitations.

Freely each one had received their Father's love, and freely they were giving it to each other.

No one was excluded from the festivities. All had their place of importance. No competition or jealousy lived here, but appreciation for the gifts and talents of one another was expressed. There was no intimidation here. All were accepted, and all were encouraged to be fully who they were created to be. No one felt like they were less important, because another excelled in a particular area. Those who were athletic were cheered on. The teachers spoke eloquently, while those listening hung on every word. Singers sang. Dancers danced. Walker's walked. Joggers jogged. All was being done with great fervor and enthusiasm.

Jesus explained: "This is what I created your world to be, a place filled with love and acceptance. Not a place where jealousy rages or infirmities destroy. What you see here in heaven will be brought to the earth at the end of the age, but you do not have to wait to receive My blessings on the earth.

"Bless one another with joy unspeakable," Jesus instructed me. "Bless marriages. Bless families with love and unity. Bless those sick and infirm with health and strength. Then you will bring heaven to the earth."

As the Lord whispered these words to me, I recalled the prayer He taught His disciples: *Father, hallowed be your name, your kingdom come. May your will be done on earth as it is in heaven (Luke 11:2).*

Then He declared: "Bring the blessings of heaven to the earth daily, for they are yours to partake of freely. Once you enter My kingdom and become citizens of heaven, all that heaven holds is yours for the taking. *I will give you the keys of the kingdom of heaven; whatever you bind on earth will be bound in heaven, and whatever you loose on earth will be loosed in heaven (Matthew 16:19).* Command those things to come to the earth, for I purchased them for you. Command health and prosperity to come, not just to you, but to all I send your way.

"Bless all, even your enemies," He reminded me. "Bless those who have hurt and wounded you and yours. All those you see enjoying heavens delights have all sinned against Me. As each one turned from their sins to Me, they were forgiven and remained blessed. Follow My example, and extend forgiveness first, then proceed to bless all extravagantly. Bless them with your words, your deeds and your declarations of prayer.

"Then," the Lord said, "you will see heaven on the earth: you'll see happy marriages, unified families, health restored and lives enjoyed. I died so that you could have My best. *I have come that they may have life, and have it to the full (John 10:10)*. Yes, I died so that mankind could possess eternal life. I also purchased life to its full measure for all, that each one would realize their potential and achieve all they were created to be."

He explained: "Do not be deceived into the falsehood that you have to wait until you come to heaven to enjoy the benefits of My kingdom. By faith, come and command those things that are not, to be. Command a blessing. Begin today to:

Ask and it will be given to you; seek and you will find; knock and the door will be open to you. For everyone who asks receives; he who seeks finds; and to him for knocks, the door will be opened (Luke 11:9–10)."

Leaving heaven today, I felt a new excitement bubbling in my being. I didn't just see the wonders and delights prepared for us in heaven. I saw a glimpse of what God wants us to receive on earth now, by accessing those blessings through prayer.

CHAPTER SIXTEEN

Ruling with His Authority

At once I was in the Spirit, and there before me was a throne in heaven with someone sitting on it. And the one who sat there had the appearance of jasper and carnelian. A rainbow, resembling an emerald, encircled the throne (Revelation 4:2-3).

In a glorious encounter with Jesus, I saw myself dressed in the jeweled coated, white gown that was covered with innumerable sparkling diamonds. Jesus warmly greeted me and escorted me into the throne room. And to my wonder, He invited me to sit on the throne next to Him.

Explaining His actions Jesus said: "You will rule on the earth, the same as you will someday rule in My kingdom. All authority in heaven and on earth has been given to Me, and I extend My authority to rule to you, My bride and friend. Do not fear or doubt that you will be equipped to rule in My place, because nothing is impossible with Me. Yes, with Me you will rule in high places. As you command in My name, in accordance with My will, everything must submit and obey. Weather disturbances must listen and heed your directives. Illnesses have to leave bodies they inhabit when you command them to go led by My Spirit. That is the key, led by My Spirit. With Me, in Me and through Me, by the power of My Spirit within you, all things will be accomplished." *To him who overcomes and does my will to the end, I will give authority over the nations (Revelation 2: 26).*

"Today I tell you, rule My daughter, My bride," Jesus declared. "Rule on the earth, as you will someday rule in heaven. Rule over the elements. Rule over all the powers of the enemy without apology. Fearlessly confront the powers who attack My children. Know who you are and who you serve. Legions of My angels will attend you. As you speak My word, they will be released to perform it. Do not doubt or fear and you will be unstoppable. Pray, speak, declare and command as I lead you, and you will see the glory of your God. When people in their ignorance seek you for freedom, instantly, you will turn them to Me."

During this encounter with Jesus, I recalled two Scripture verses that proclaim Jesus' authority:

All authority in heaven and on earth has been given to me. Therefore go and make disciples of all nations... (Matthew 28:18–19). And also: When Jesus had called the Twelve together, he gave them power and authority to drive out all demons and to cure diseases, and he sent them out to preach the kingdom of God and to heal the sick (Luke 9:1–2).

When Jesus died on the cross and rose again, He defeated Satan. No longer does Satan have the legal right to rule the earth. Now the rightful King is Jesus Christ, and we are His chosen ambassadors. He has called His followers to implement His victory and command the forces of darkness to let His people go. The job of the church is to pick up the weapons of our warfare and demolish those strongholds that Satan erects in people's lives. By using the name of Jesus, applying the blood of the Lamb, praying in the spirit, forgiving and loving our enemies and declaring the word of God, we can implement Jesus' glorious victory. (See Ephesians 6:10–18).

This directive to rule and to assert the authority of Jesus Christ over evil is for all Christians. Though the Lord spoke these words to me about ruling over the forces of darkness, they apply to all of us. These words spoken by Jesus just before He left the earth to sit on the right hand of His Father in heaven make that very clear. All who believe have been given the authority by Jesus Christ to command demons and the forces of darkness to release God's people.

> *And these signs will accompany those who believe: in my name they will drive out demons; they will speak in new tongues... they will place their hands on sick people, and they will get well (Mark 16:17–18).*

The Lord explained clearly who we truly are and the power He has given us, when He said:

> *I tell you the truth, anyone who has faith in me will do what I have been doing. He will do even greater things than these, because I am going to the Father. And I will do whatever you ask in my name, so that the Son may bring glory to the Father. You may ask me for anything in my name, and I will do it (John 14:12–14).*

Revisiting The Throne Room

To my great delight, today I saw my heavenly Father sitting on His throne. I didn't see Him clearly, but I did see Him more clearly than ever before. His throne was enormous and elaborate. He welcomed me like I was special, someone He delighted visiting with. As I drew near, He extended His beautiful, ornate, gold scepter. I touched the end of it, and as He beckoned me, I sat beside my God and King.

In that special place, I began to ask Him to help my friends, relatives, ministry concerns and my nation. I was reminded of Queen Esther as she went before King Xerxes. (See Esther 5:1–3.) She went on behalf of her nation. I knew my God was showing me that, just like Queen Esther was able to get help and deliverance from certain destruction for her people, I could get the same from my King, my God.

Then, as we sat together, my Father handed me His scepter and told me He trusted me with it, the rod of his authority. Mordecai got

King Xerxes' signet ring, but He explained that I was being given my King's scepter to wield:

"Only those I trust are given this privilege, to exert My authority, to command in My name and to speak on My behalf. A new level of authority has been granted to you, and to those like you, because each of you can be trusted, for I have seen your hearts."

He exclaimed, "In obedience, you have spoken what I have commanded without withholding the word for fear of the consequences! You have destroyed fear of man and honored Me. This is your reward, for I do reward those who diligently serve Me with obedient hearts. Every demon who sees the scepter will submit to it. Whatever I ask you to declare will have the sting of My power on it. Doors will open when you tell them to. Demons will flee or be silenced. The sick will rise and be healed. The blind will see.

"Do not fear," He said firmly, "for My Spirit will guide you how and when to wield My scepter. You know My Spirit. Just listen and obey as each of you has in the past. But now you will see far greater results, for you have been promoted to a new level of spiritual authority (see Matthew 28:18–19)."

Not only was I given the golden scepter, but I also received a new garment, a beautiful gem embossed, long dress with shoes to match. I knew this outfit represented a fresh new anointing. All the gifts of the Holy Spirit were increased and all the gifts and callings strengthened, so I, and those like me, would be more effective and more fruitful for His kingdoms sake!

Jesus said to them, "I tell you the truth, at the renewal of all things, when the Son if Man sits on his glorious throne, you who have followed me will also sit on twelve thrones, judging the twelve tribes of Israel" (Matthew 19:28).

CHAPTER SEVENTEEN

Soaking in His Presence

At once I was in the spirit, and there before me was a throne in heaven with someone sitting on it (Revelation 4:2).

Days later, I was back in the spirit in a very delightful place. Instantly I saw myself in this interactive vision, lying on the lush, deep green, grass in heaven. The Lord was lying beside me. Looking up, I noted that the once blue sky had transformed into a vast glorious rainbow, just like the magnificent rainbow I had seen months before in the sky over the Father's home. I recalled that John reported seeing this very same thing: *A rainbow, resembling an emerald, encircled the throne (Revelation 4:3).*

But above all this was something even more astonishing; rain fell from the sky and continually soaked us. *He will be like rain falling on a mown field, like showers watering the earth (Psalm 72:6).* This was not an ordinary rain. For nothing in heaven is ordinary. The rain I felt pour down out of the rainbow covered sky was liquid love. Literally, the love of God was dancing on me like the gentle steps of a tiny kitten walking on a sleeping child. Unlike rain on the earth, this heavenly rain was warm, gentle but strong. Instead of hitting me and soaking my skin and clothing, heaven's rain immediately went into my being. I was being filled with the love of God like we fill our cars with fuel. Every pore in my body drank in love. As I responded to this outpouring of divine love with ovations of my love, the intensity of the rain increased. Love magnified!

I asked, "Lord, am I at the throne of God?"

Immediately my Friend responded, "Heaven is the throne of God and the earth His footstool."

My spiritual eyes opened wider, and I saw things too glorious to recount. I was lying at the feet of God under a magnificent rainbow, drenched in His tremendous love, with Jesus lying on the grass laughing beside me. I could only see a shadow or wisp of my Father. What I saw brought me to tears. I was like a speck of dust in size in comparison to the enormity of our heavenly Father. He stood up and walked away and was taller than I could see. Our God is a majestic God! Far too mighty for us to imagine or perceive. His Majesty reaches to the highest heavens. In the shadow, in the midst, I saw a smile and knew God was smiling down on me.

My Lord whispered in my ear, "See why I was able to go to the cross."

His cry became mine: "Father, whatever you want, I will do. Father, I am yours. I will serve your Majesty. I will bow before your might. I will follow you and trust your will for my life. I will go to the cross in my life. I will deny myself and die to my desires. I will live for you, my God!"

Holy, holy, holy is the Lord God Almighty, who was, and is, and is to come. You are worthy, our Lord and our God, to receive glory and honor and power, for you created all things, and by your will they were created and have their being (Revelation 4: 8, 11).

Then I heard, "Anyone can come and lay at My feet. All are invited but few come. I am accessible to all." Though my God was enormous, vast beyond comprehension, He was close. Mighty but gentle. His voice was soft as a whisper but strong like the roar of many waters.

Tenderly He spoke: "Tell My people to seek My face. Tell them to turn from their wicked ways. Tell them to pray, and I will hear them, and I will heal their land. This is not the hour when the earth will be destroyed. Rather, it is the hour when I desire to pour out My

Spirit, not My wrath, upon all flesh. Pray, fast, seek My face and you will live to see the glory of your God revealed."

Lying on the grass, under the rainbow canopy above, with the rain of His Spirit pouring down on me, He explained that the rain doesn't just soak into us and fill us with His love, but that its work is twofold.

Besides equipping us, it cleanses us and purifies us of all that defiles us, so that we can be transparent. That is His goal, to make us transparent so that when people see us, they can see His presence shining through us. All that clouds, or covers over us, will be washed away as we soak in His presence at the throne of God. All are invited, and the way there has been made accessible by the blood of Jesus. Soaking in His presence cleanses us and equips us so that the image of Jesus can be fashioned in our lives. (See Revelation 4:3; Genesis 9:8–17.)

While looking up at the rainbow, I thought of the rainbow God placed in the sky after the great flood (see Isaiah 54:9-12). The rainbow was a sign of an agreement that God made with Noah to never destroy the earth by a flood again. I knew I was lying under a rainbow of covenant: the new covenant which promised that God would be my God, and I would be His child. (See Jeremiah 31:33.) He would lead me, teach me and convict me. I would look to Him for all I needed and not to any man for anything.

Jesus paid a tremendous price so that we could be partakers in this new covenant. He died on the cross and shed His blood to satisfy this agreement between God and man. Now we can come boldly to the throne of grace and mercy. The mercy seat is accessible to all! The curtain keeping us out of the throne was torn in two. (See Luke 23:45.) Now all can come into God's throne room and seek His presence; none are exempt. All can come through the blood of the Lamb. Jesus explained:

"So few come and take full advantage of what I purchased for them. All they need can be obtained at My Father's feet. The throne of grace and mercy is where healing is found. This is where My Father provides for His children. He beckons them, 'Come. Come; for the way has been made clear by My Son. Come and receive My best.'

"But few listen. Few respond. Oh, how different their lives would be if they would just respond and come. I am a big God—mighty in all My ways. And nothing is impossible for Me. As you come before Me, trust Me to take care of all that concerns you, for I am able! Just ask, believe and receive. For I will withhold no good thing from My children who earnestly seek Me. Yes, I will be found by all who yearn after My presence. In My presence is the fullness of joy. Joy escapes those who are sick and in pain, or weak and forlorn. Those weary with troubles feel no joy. I am the lifter of the heads of My children. All they need to bring them true joy is found at the foot of My throne. Healing, deliverance, blessings and abundance: all are found at My feet. Just come. Seek Me, and you will find life, the fullness of life, joy unspeakable."

Let us then approach the throne of grace with confidence, so that we may receive mercy and find grace to help us in our time of need (Hebrews 4:16).

Therefore, brothers, since we have confidence to enter the Most Holy Place by the blood of Jesus, by a new and living way opened for us through the curtain, that is, his body, and since we have a great priest over the house of God, let us draw near to God with a sincere heart in full assurance of faith, having our hearts sprinkled to cleanse us from a guilty conscience and having our bodies washed with pure water (Hebrews 10:19–22)

He concluded our visit with these memorable words: "My presence, My Spirit, My glory is all one and the same. When you have My presence, you have the best I could give anyone.

My presence convicts, cleanses and empowers all who receive Me wholeheartedly."

Heaven's Amusement Park

"Today I tell you to relax and enjoy the life I have given you," I heard as I sat before my Friend. "I do not want you to work continuously. When you do that, as so many of My servants have in the past, you will wear out the body and soul I have blessed you with. Yes, I say soul, for your soul, or emotions, are restored as you relax and laugh. Remember it is the joy of the Lord that brings you strength and restores your soul. Relax, laugh and enjoy those things and people I have surrounded you with."

On this special day, the Lord brought me high, past all the clouds in the sky into the spirit realm to heaven. To My utter amazement, He led me into a fantastic amusement park. The first thing I saw amongst the colorful, lavishly decorated rides was an enormous Ferris Wheel. Like a gleeful child, My Lord laughed heartily and invited me to come and ride with Him. From His demeanor, I knew He couldn't wait to share this totally enjoyable ride with me. Sitting side-by-side, laughing and relaxing together, the brightly lit ride swung in the air and brought us high above the surrounding rides.

Looking down, I saw order and balance. I saw no flaws in anything or anyone. I watched as colorful clowns on stilts greeted many happy children arriving for their day of fun. Popcorn, cotton candy in many delightful colors, candy apples were just a few of the snacks they ate. Elaborate booths lined the walkway inviting all who passed by to come and try their skills to win a prize. Laughter abounded. Joy was everywhere.

Then our ride came to a halt. With great enjoyment, I stepped off the platform and followed my Friend as He led me safely to another ride. This was a large dunking tank. Together we climbed up the golden ladder and sat on the gem studded platform above the water. Then someone threw a ball and hit the target right on its mark. Down we went, laughing all the way. Instantly we landed in water that felt like a warm liquid love. Together we swam—as the tank was actually a very large swimming pool. With each stroke I felt energized and refreshed. A new strength seemed to flow through my being.

Once we reach the end of the pool, we climbed out and sat together under a fruit tree on a grassy knoll. The Lord offered me a piece of fruit. The flavor was sumptuous, unlike anything I had ever eaten. Every one of my taste buds rejoiced. Heavens food cannot be compared to any we have here on the earth.

Once we had rested from our swim, we jumped up together and hand-in-hand went off to spend the afternoon going from ride to ride in heaven's amusement park. Roller coasters, aerial rides, train rides through ornate castles: all were beautiful beyond description. Each one was thoroughly exciting; some were very daring, yet safe and comfortable. The best part of all was enjoying it while gazing into the loving eyes of my best Friend. His strong arms around my shoulders and His hearty laugh taught me much.

I learned that the Lord wants us to live balanced lives. Even in heaven there is a time and a place to relax and have fun. Here, too, on the earth, the Lord wants us to stop from laboring continually and spend time just having fun with Him beside us. As we stop to smell the roses and enjoy our lives, He will come and lavish us with His loving presence. He does not want us to grow weary in well doing. We will accomplish this by allowing Him to lead us by His Spirit to just relax and enjoy those things He has brought into our lives.

For some of us there is a park or the ocean nearby, a stream or pond waiting for us to fish in, friends and family members to enjoy, or a long awaited vacation for us to take. These are all provided by our Master and loving Father and quite necessary for us to restore our souls and strengthen our bodies.

He reminded me that, "This is what life is like when you living in union with Me. There will be times of refreshing and times of great excitement. You will experience new delights daily; for I am not a boring God."

CHAPTER EIGHTEEN

Impacting Encounters in Heaven

In the year that King Uzziah died, I saw the Lord seated on a throne, high and exalted, and this train of his robe filled the temple (Isaiah 6:1).

In an instant, I was in my Father's house. He made it very apparent that He was happy to see me. He explained that He had been waiting patiently for me to push through the distractions that kept me from entering into the spirit realm. Preoccupation with many things and people had hindered me from encountering Him.

"It is only in that secret place far from the distractions of the world where you will find Me. That is why I ask My people to seek Me. There is a letting go of the external and a seeking after He who resides deep within the heart of man, that is required to truly encounter Me. Come; let us get apart together, for I have much to show you today. I have been calling you, but My voice was faint. The voice of all that concerns you has overshadowed My still small voice;" He stated as we walked out of the throne room to the stairway that led into His private study.

There was the familiar comfortable, overstuffed couch and the large windows overlooking the world. My Father laughed as we sat down. A gleam sparkled in His eyes. Curiosity filled my wondering thoughts. What was my Father thinking that caused Him such amusement? Silently I sat and looked at His form and into His eyes.

I waited, knowing He was sure to reveal His thoughts to me. What could be giving Him such joy?

Suddenly the joy that swept over me was infiltrated with the same joy I saw on my Father. This joy was so delightful that I could not keep from laughing. As I laughed and laughed, His thoughts merged with mine. I knew that my heavenly Father was so happy because He delighted in doing good to me. Instantly I saw that many of the things and people I had prayed for had been helped. Answered prayers marched before me in a steady stream. I saw each one of my children helped; friends were strengthened and set free from those things that were oppressing them; leaders were given wisdom and the help they needed. On and on they passed before my mind. Each one was blessed by God.

The more I observed, the harder I laughed. My joy was complete. So many were helped, because my Father had heard every prayer and answered each one. This gave Him great joy. To bless His children is the delight of God.

"I am laughing," He explained, "not only for those things that I have done for you. I am laughing because I know what I am going to do in the days ahead. It brings Me delight knowing how happy you will be when you see those things you have cried out for accomplished; even those issues that you didn't ask for, but desired, will be given to you."

He continued to teach me: "In the Parable of the Lost Son (see Luke 15:11-32), when the boy arrived home and fell into his father's embrace, what did he receive? All he asked for, yes, but much more as well. He wanted a roof over his head, food to eat and to be received as a servant. But what was he given? He received more than he even desired. He was given new clothes, shoes, a ring, a great party and restored as a son to his father.

"You have never left Me. How much more will I do for My faithful children. Over and above what you could think or ask is what I'm going to bring into your lives in this hour. That is why I laugh. I have been waiting to see you, so I could tell you this good news. My joy has been full. With great longing I have awaited your arrival, so I could tell you what I have in store for you and for My faithful ones, My daughter."

He explained: "I am a God of second, third, fourth... chances. Yes, I do discipline, and when My people repent, I restore. Nothing pleases Me more than to bless those who humble themselves before Me. Friendships are quickly restored when My people return to Me, and all that was lost in the season of rebellion is returned quickly! That is who I am; a God who waits with open arms for My children to run back to Me, so that I can pour out on their lives, and the lives of their loved ones, the fullness of My benefits.

"I will withhold no good thing from those who love and serve Me. For those who remain faithful, all I have belongs to them. If I will so freely give of My best to My returning sons and daughters, how much more will I bestow upon those who never leave Me or forsake My ways. Know this, I am a God who loves to forgive, who lived and died to forgive! No sin is to great, nor any sinner to vile for Me to absolve, nor is any situation too difficult for Me to redeem."

Shadows of His Glory

The Son is the radiance of God's glory and the exact representation of his being, sustaining all things by his powerful word (Hebrews 1:3).

Another wonderful day, while in prayer, the Lord led me into the Father's house by the bridge onto the gem, stepping-stone path. The stones were very large, made of different colored gemstones. I looked down at one, and it's shine was so brilliant and its texture so smooth that I could see the reflection of Jesus' face and mine smiling, laughing, cheek to cheek.

After enjoying this moment together, we advanced to the front door. Instantly the door responded to our touch and opened. Inside we saw the great crowd of witnesses; millions surrounding His throne. All I wanted to do was lay at the Father's feet. I was content to be His foot rest, but the Father would not. As I attempted to lie at His feet, He greeted me and invited me to come and sit beside Him. His welcome was sincere and filled with loving acceptance.

Then He got up and invited me to follow Him. Tenderly my Father led me out into His glorious flower garden. His plants and rosebushes were magnificent, so large and full, and each flower so plush. Hanging in the midst of a grove of red and yellow roses was a garden swing. There we sat: the Father beside me, the wonderful Son of God on His other side and His precious Holy Spirit on the other side of me. The Father explained that my level of faith allowed me to see the Godhead.

Though I could not see them clearly, I saw their form and new who each one was; I heard, "Whenever you visit with either of us, you visit with all three, because We are one."

Looking around at this elegant scene, my eyes rested upon gold brocade cushions and roses climbing up the gold chains that the swing was suspended from. Overhead I saw red, yellow and pink roses that danced above our heads. What amazed me the most was the carpet of flowers that lay at our feet. I asked the Father, "How did you do that?"

"Nothing is impossible for me," He laughed.

Then I remembered seeing a similar sight the day before while walking with my daughter. A gentleman was working on his flower garden near the beach we were visiting. He had planted multicolored flowers, and his flower bed carpeted the entire garden that surrounded his house.

My Father then explained how He reveals Himself to us in unimaginable ways:

"Yes, what you saw yesterday was a little glimpse of what I have placed in My kingdom. Look with eyes of faith, and you will see shadows of My glory displayed on the earth. All creation reflects the wonders of the mystery of the Trinity. Yes, look and you will see the love, unity, beauty and power of your God displayed, for I do want you to know Me.

"When I created mankind, not only did I make them in My image, but I made them to know Me, to love Me and to serve Me. Yes, I still desire man to know Me, though we were separated by sin. If we are not allowed to walk and talk together, then I will still find a way to reveal myself to My children. I want them to know Me, walk with Me and be My friends.

"Look with expectancy. Open your eyes, and see My beauty. See My Majesty. Look throughout creation, and My Spirit will show you who I am. Do not allow anything to limit your experience of who I am nor limit your knowledge. Creation reflects My glory.

"When you see kindness and generosity displayed, know that you are seeing but a shadow of My goodness. Lift your understanding to know that what you are seeing simply reflects a small part of My nature. I did make man in My image (see Genesis 1:26–27). See My affection in those who lovingly embrace and accept you. See My gentleness as others extend a gentle touch to you, especially when you need a gentle touch. That is who I am, a gentle touch during tempest tossed times. See My smile as it beams from the face of those who admire you, for that is who I am. I am a Father who deeply admires My children and who values each and every accomplishment.

"All creation reflects My glory! *The heavens declare the glory of God; the skies proclaim the work of his hands (Psalm 19:1).* A soaring eagle reflects My power; a thrashing hippo, My great strengths; a prancing kitten, My dexterity; a newborn chick, My softness. Look and see. It is the work of My Spirit to reveal who I am to mankind, but you must listen. You must look with expectant eyes of faith. Then you will behold the glory of your God.

"Many cry out to see My glory, but they look for Me where I cannot be found. They look in the places where religion resides. I am not there. They look for Me in the stale and the stuffy places of life, but that is not who I am. I am life. I am joy. I am gentleness. I am power. I am vibrancy.

"The work of the church is to unveil Me to others. Present Me properly! The work of My friends is to complete the work of My Son, to reveal the Father to the world. Show them My true glory, My real goodness. Religious activities are fake and do not reveal who I am.

"From now on, when you encounter people don't focus on their flaws! Look for My glory displayed in them. Look and you will find Me there. If you stay focused on the imperfections, you won't find perfection there."

Finally, brothers, whatever is true, whatever is noble, whatever is right, whatever is pure, whatever is lovely, whatever is admirable–if anything is excellent or praiseworthy–think about such things (Philippians 4:8).

He coaxed me, "Don't miss Me for I am truly hidden in every heart. Mankind was made in My image."

Heavens Glory Brought to the Earth

One sunny afternoon while in the spirit realm, I found myself sitting beside my Father in His comfortable den. I heard:

"Everything in heaven reflects My glory and declares who I am: The unity of the Trinity, the devotion of My Son, the power of My Holy Spirit. My will is that mankind would see My glory on earth, for just as heaven reflects My glory, so does the earth. All were made by My hand, and all reflect the qualities of their Creator. I have placed My stamp of authority on each and everything I spoke into existence. Yes, I created man in My image, but I also created all things to reflect part of My nature.

"The eyes of mankind have been blinded to My glory by the powers of darkness," He said. "In the days ahead, those blinders will be lifted and men will see My glory reflected everywhere they look. Suddenly they will see, and suddenly they will know who I am. In this knowledge, a great devotion to Me will evolve.

My Father continued to teach me: "All creation reflects the glory of its Creator (see Psalm 72:19). The more I am revealed and known, the more I will be loved and served. That is why the enemy's device is to blind the eyes of men from seeing Me. He does this by keeping them self-focused, which eventually brings depression, disillusionment and every other evil."

He had my full attention when He explained: "Look at Cain and Abel (see Genesis 4:1–16). Cain was totally self-absorbed. He looked upon his brother with a jealous eye. Hatred replaced love. Cain knew Me. We walked and talk together. He saw My glory. Instead of keeping his eyes fixed on his God, he saw only himself.

"Selfishness is a trap and a tool of the enemy. He uses it well to draw men away from me. Once we are separated, then he lures them into a lifestyle of sin. There are many Cains alive today. Jealousy and envy prod them into murderous acts. Many want what their brothers have without paying the price that their brothers paid to obtain their wealth.

"Abel was devoted to Me. He paid the price for My favor by his obedient friendship. Self-absorbed, Cain wanted that same favor but didn't want to earn it by truly loving Me. There are no shortcuts to obtain My glory, but there are stumbling blocks–the biggest being self-absorption.

"That is why I command My children to worship Me. Worship exalts another—Me-- and negates self. Worship brings My presence and diminishes selfishness. Worship causes men to look outward. Worship Me in all circumstances, then I will show up, and I will be glorified instead of the god of self.

My Father concluded His teaching: "That is why I placed so many signs of My glory on the earth. They serve as reminders of who I am. The more men are absorbed in My presence, the more they will reflect My glory. Self-absorbed people reflect their own glory, which cannot be compared to the glory of God (see 2 Corinthians 3:17–18). Let creation remind you of who I am and coax you to get apart with Me."

Cain, who was filled with pride, came into God's presence with an offering of fruit from his land, while Abel came in humility. In order to present his offering of the fat portions from some of the firstborn of his flock, Abel had to shed blood. This shedding of blood was a sign of his sorrow for his sins. Abel came knowing he was not perfect, but that God was. Cain came in pride, not in obedience and humility, therefore, his offering was not acceptable.

In the parable of the Pharisee and the Tax Collector in Luke 18:9–14, Jesus taught about two men who came into the Temple to pray. The Pharisee stood in God's presence and thanked God that he was not like the tax collector or other men: robbers, evildoers, adulterers. He declared that he tithed and fasted twice a week. He thought his own efforts justified him. The tax collector came in humility: beat his breast, lowered his head and asked God to have mercy on him, a sinner. Jesus declared that the tax collector left justified, because he admitted that he was a sinner and asked for

God's forgiveness and help. The humble tax collector was blessed and had God's approval just like Abel did.

> *Humble yourselves before the Lord, and he will lift you up (James 4:10).*

CHAPTER NINETEEN

A Shadow of the Kingdom of Heaven

Then I heard every creature in heaven and on earth and under the earth and on the sea, and all that is in them, singing: "To him who sits on the throne and to the lamb be praise and honor and glory and power, for ever and ever!" (Revelation 5:13).

The familiar feeling of His overshadowing love engulfed me as I sat before the Lord in deep prayer. Peering into the spirit, I saw myself flying rapidly with Jesus over the earth. *The Spirit lifted me up between earth and heaven and in visions of God he took me to Jerusalem (Ezekiel 8:3).*

From a distance, I saw its incredible beauty: Snow covered mountains and valleys shimmering in the bright sunlight; then a region filled with lush green trees and fertile foliage; next a region where trees lay dormant waiting for the warmth of spring to touch them and bring them back to vibrant life; and last, a tropical land brimming over with palm trees, soft breezes and glistening waterways. This was the magnificent earth that I gazed upon that He made for His children to dwell on.

As soon as our spiritual flight over the earth ended, He brought me to the summit of the Mountain of Intimacy where He often takes me to sit and talk with Him.

The Seasons in Heaven Revealed

Thinking that He was going to speak to me about the earth, I was quite surprised when He began to teach me about heaven:

"Heaven does not compare in its detail, or in its majestic size, to the earth. Just as you have seasons on the earth, in heaven, too, there are seasons. Those that love the winter months and the delights of freshly fallen snow and glistening ice will find them here. Others who, like you, enjoy the warmer climates will enjoy it to their hearts delight. My world is not boring nor is it inclement. Never is the sun too hot or the snow too cold for the senses of those who dwell forever in My paradise. I delight to make My children happy. To see each one enjoy the dazzling crystal-like snow and the beauty of My lush gardens gives Me great pleasure.

"The earth," He explained, "is but a faint reflection of My kingdom. All the beauty and glamour of the earth is like a shadow compared to the splendor and the size of My kingdom."

Expounding upon His sovereignty He continued: "Don't forget, I am the King. All that I create reflects My power, My love and My greatness. My kingdom is not influenced by any, only by Me. Sin can cast no shadow of death or darkness on My land nor can it mar the infinite beauty here. Far greater than you could ever expect is the place I have prepared for those who follow My Son. Enlarge your vision, and let your expectations grow. I am a big God, and what I made for My children reflects who I am."

Above the expanse over their heads was what looked like a throne of sapphire, and high above on the throne was a figure like that of a man. I saw that from what appeared to be his waist up he looked like glowing metal, as if full of fire, and that from there down he looked like fire; and brilliant light surrounding him. Like the appearance of a rainbow in the clouds on a rainy day, so was the radiance around him (Ezekiel 1:26-28).

A Third Visit to the Hall of Miracles

A few weeks after this delightful encounter, to my utter delight, the Lord brought me back into my favorite place in heaven, the Hall of Miracles. Finding myself standing in the spirit on the gleaming gold floor, I immediately ran and peered into the rooms that lined the long hallway. To my amazement, I observed that most of the rooms were empty of their contents.

The Lord explained that those things that I had seen previously in these rooms had been released to the earth. Some of the hearts waiting to be given to those who would receive a new passion for Jesus had been sent to hungry men, women and children. The room where I saw the sign of the outpouring of His Spirit was alive with activity. His Spirit had been poured out on those who had asked for the outpouring of the Holy Spirit. Their faith and hunger for more of Him had brought some of heaven into their lives.

Angels were dancing and rejoicing with great enthusiasm. His messengers who had, in obedience to the Father, brought the contents of these rooms to the earth could not contain their joy at what the Lord was doing on the earth. Men were falling in love with their King and Lord. Holiness was being embraced as a lifestyle. The brokenhearted, lonely and forlorn were healed and were rejoicing as they had never before. Marriages and broken relationships were restored. New ones were established. Lives were changed and the angels were rejoicing because their God was well pleased.

In an instant, I saw the other places I had visited in heaven. These regions were ablaze with excitement as well. All heaven was rejoicing with their King. The power He so longed for His people to have was sent to the earth through the great outpouring of the Holy Spirit. The work He began on earth was now bearing its fruit. Similar to the revival that broke out at Pentecost, the birth of the Church, souls were being saved, lives restored, health returned. All heaven felt the same joy that was in the heart of their King because they were one with Him. This was not a manufactured enthusiasm, but it was a sincere, genuine excitement emanated from everything in heaven. Just like I felt the Father's love pour out of every object in heaven, now I felt joy and excitement pouring forth, too.

As I cried out for more of that same joyful expectation that flooded heaven to fill my heart I heard: "That is why I have brought you here today. I am releasing faith into your heart that will allow joyful excitement and enthusiastic expectation to fill you as it fills heaven. This faith will draw the things of heaven to the earth: My love, health, joy, unity, kindness and patience. Faith fills heaven because all here know what I will do. The hour is at hand, and all heaven rejoices with Me that My will shall be done on earth as it is in heaven."

Leaving Heaven to Return to the Earth

> *...I saw the Lord seated on a throne, high and exalted, and the train of his robe filled the temple. Above him were six seraphs, each with six wings... And they were calling to one another: "Holy, holy, holy is the Lord Almighty; the whole earth is full of his glory" (Isaiah 6:1–3).*

Again I was in the spirit in the presence of the Lord, and to my great pleasure, I had the diamond laden, long, white gown on. Its elegance was unmatched by anything I'd ever seen. The Lord told me that each glistening diamond represented a deed that was done on earth for Him: a prayer prayed, a kind word spoken, on and on. The largest diamonds and those in the most significant places on the dress were prayers offered for those who had injured me or even hated me. Obedience gleaned an enormous reward!

Far greater than the incredible beauty of this dress, the majestic glory of my surroundings, the gold floor I stood on and the palatial rooms about us was the awesome presence of Jesus as He stood looking upon me. The overwhelming love that poured out of His eyes far surpassed all the elegance and opulence of my surroundings. Being bathed in His loving acceptance took my breath away and caused everything else about me to diminish in its importance. He was all I needed and all I wanted. Nothing else mattered in this place but being loved by Him. Being loved by Love Himself was the greatest gift of all, one I could take with me back to the realm of the natural world.

My Mansion in Heaven

While absorbing His great love for me, suddenly He opened my eyes to see in the spirit more clearly. Peering into the distance my Lord took me by the hand and brought me to the entrance to a magnificent mansion. He explained that this was the home that He has prepared for me. Like a little child running through a toy store, my eyes darted throughout this exquisite home. In awe and in great delight, I saw solid gold fixtures in the many of the rooms, elegant draperies and delightful furniture in every room. Many of the walls were decorated with sparkling jewels; marble and other exquisite materials that I had never seen on the earth were found in most of the rooms. Adding to my great delight, an enormous, heated pool filled another room. This swimming pool had the same water in it that flows from the throne of God. Anyone who enters it is immediately soaked in the love of God.

Though the beauty of this house captivated me more than I can describe, I was more deeply impressed by the profound love and devotion our Father has for each of us. Only an enormous love could prompt anyone, even our God, to prepare such a magnificent mansion for each of us. Observing the twinkle in His eye, I was overjoyed at how pleased it made Him to bring so much happiness to just one of His friends.

Seeing the glories that have been prepared by our Father for His children is a joy that is difficult to describe. Leaving them behind to return to the things of the earth is easy to bear, because each and every time I'm there, He fills me with His love, the greatest treasure heaven offers.

My dress hangs in my closet in heaven awaiting my home-coming, but His love is mine to treasure in my heart and share with all I meet on the earth.

Conclusion

Enjoy the Sweetness of His Presence

The Son is the radiance of God's glory and the exact representation of his being, sustaining all things by his powerful word (Hebrews 1:3)

My Lord handed me a piece of honeycomb that was dripping with honey. I knew that the words that He was going to speak would be sweet and would nourish my soul. He began our visit with this exhortation:

"You have seen heaven and hell. Yes, you have walked the corridors of heaven and the trenches of hell and seen the glories and riches I have prepared for those who love and serve Me, along with the horrors and cruelty the enemy has stored up for those who serve him. Spiteful and filled with malice are the benefit's the evil one has prepared as a reward for his followers. If My children knew the truth, very few would freely choose to follow him or embrace his sinful ways."

His Glory Will Rain Upon the Earth

Looking into the spirit, as was my custom when we met, I saw liquid gold raining down from the heavens and passing through billowy white clouds.

He declared: "Everything in heaven is filled with My love, and the rain of My glory is no different. Open yourself to be washed in the liquid gold of My love. Immediately you will be transformed. Love begets love. The more love you receive, the more you will be able to give to others. Be like Me. Pour My love out on others, as they open themselves up to receive."

He explained that the days ahead will be filled with the same glory that saturates everything in heaven. For those who believe in Him and faithfully obey His directives, there will be wonderful times of enjoying His love, His power and His great glory as they come to the earth. Miracles will be a natural outcome of this great outpouring of His majesty and His love. The long awaited revival is on its way!

Sadly the Lord showed me that Satan, too, has a plan. His scheme is to bring worldwide destruction and severe suffering to the world. From recent tragic events, this, too, appears to have begun.

But above all, I believe that we are seeing signs that the tremendous revival is already beginning. The gentle rain that announces an approaching storm has been felt. Reports of many people experiencing the glory of God, like never before, are heard in the USA and in many lands. My prayer is that all will partake of His wonderful benefits and allow the Holy Spirit to turn them fully to Jesus before it is too late. *O Israel, put your hope in the Lord, for with the Lord is unfailing love...(Psalm 130:7).*

There Is Hope for You

The hour is late, but it is not too late for individuals to turn to Jesus. All who call upon His name will be saved. Do not miss the opportunity to embrace Him and know the comfort of being His. Whatever happens on the earth, in the years to come, there is a hereafter. Heaven could be your home eternally, if you make the free choice to receive His forgiveness for your sins and embrace the salvation He purchased for you on Calvary. Faith in Him and in His love for you will change your eternal destiny forever.

For all those that are not sure if your eternal home is in heaven, here is a prayer for you to pray, so that you can know of a certainty that you belong to Him:

Jesus, I believe that you are the Son of God. I believe that you left heaven and came to the earth to pay the full price for my sins by dying on the cross. I am sorry for all of the sins I have committed during my life. Please forgive me. I renounce Satan and all his works. I accept the sacrifice you made for me and the price you paid for my sins to be forgiven forever. I believe that you rose from the dead, and with you I can live again in Eternity. I give you my life and promise to follow you and embrace your ways. Please come and live in my heart and fill me with your Holy Spirit.

If you chose to sincerely pray this prayer, you can be assured that no matter what comes upon the earth in the years to come, He will take care of you forever, here and in heaven.

In order to carry out the commitment you have made to follow Jesus, a few things would greatly benefit you. Get a Bible, and read it daily. Talk with your new Friend who lives within you. He loves to listen and will speak to you, if you listen carefully. Find other Christians to spend time with, and finally, ask Him to lead you to a church where you can grow in His grace.

Don't fear the future. It's in His hands and so are you!

Author Bio

Donna Rigney and her husband, Jack, are pastors of a non-denominational church in North central Florida. An author, successful playwright and inspirational speaker, Donna also started a missionary work in Croatia. She currently serves on the advisory board of a youth detention facility where she ministers at a mid-week service. Her prophetic books and motivating messages effectively resound with a call for intimacy with God.

To contact the author please write Donna Rigney at:
His Heart Ministries International
Box 5042 Salt Springs, Florida 32134
Internet address: hisheartinternational@yahoo.com

Please include your testimony or help received from her books when you write. Your prayer requests are welcome.

Author Bio

Read Donna Rigney's Book

Abused By The Church

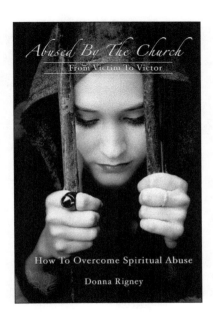

The innocent and the deceived will be set free and empowered as they read this life changing book. For far too long people have experienced abuse in the church and have been assigned to a place of secrecy and shame. Hurt and disillusioned, multitudes have left the church. Their tragic stories are related in *Abused By The Church* so that healing, restoration and reform can take place. It is the time for genuine change--for justice to rule in the place of tyranny. The hour is at hand for Christ's wounded ones to be healed and restored to the Church. Victims will become victors!

Abused By The Church ISBN 978-1-61579-4454 is available at Amazon.com and other fine retailers. It is also available as an e-book.

CPSIA information can be obtained
at www.ICGtesting.com
Printed in the USA
FSHW020336020221